Fingal's Cave, the Poems of Ossian, and Celtic Christianity

Fingal, the great initiate hero, one of the out-standing spiritually awakened individualities of the Gaelic world, guided the destiny of his people from the earliest times onward. His name was given long ago to that unique wonder of the natural world, known as Fingal's Cave, located on the island of Staffa in the Scottish Hebrides. Fingal's fame was sung by his son, the blind bard Ossian, often called the Homer of the ancient Scottish North.

PAUL M. ALLEN
and JOAN deRIS ALLEN

Fingal's Cave,
the Poems of Ossian,
and Celtic Christianity

CONTINUUM • NEW YORK

1999
The Continuum Publishing Company
370 Lexington Avenue
New York, NY 10017

Copyright © 1999 by Joan deRis Allen

Printed in the United States of America

Library of Congress Cataloging-in-Publication Data

Allen, Paul Marshall.
  Fingal's Cave, the poems of Ossian, and Celtic Christianity / Paul M. Allen and Joan
deRis Allen.
      p.   cm.
  Includes bibliographical references.
  ISBN 0-8264-1144-4 (alk. paper)
    1. Macpherson, James, 1736–1796. Ossian.   2. Finn MacCumhaill, 3rd cent.—
Legends—History and criticism.   3. Literary forgeries and mystifications—History—
18th century.   4. Fingal's Cave (Scotland)—In literature.   5. Macpherson, James,
1736–1796—Influence.   6. Ossian, 3rd cent.—In literature.   7. Bards and bardism in
literature.   8. Mythology, Celtic, in literature.   9. Fingal's Cave (Scotland)
10. Celts—Religion. I. Allen, Joan deRis, 1931–   .   II. Title.
PR3544.A86 1999
821'.6—dc21   98-53760
                                                                            CIP

Contents

Fingal, a sketch by Philipp Otto Runge,
1804, Hamburg Kunsthalle.

Illustrations

Preface
Changing Human Consciousness

 In the later half of the eighteenth century and in course of the nineteenth, powerful impulses from the spiritual world manifested themselves in the earthly sphere in a number of ways. One of these took the form of the publication of a book entitled *Fingal—An Ancient Epic Poem in Six Books Together with Several Other Poems* composed by Ossian, the son of Fingal, translated from the Gaelic language by James Macpherson. First published in London 1762, this single event evoked a mighty response, producing a tremendous impression, not only in Great Britain but in many parts of Europe, and in the Americas as well. This book has long been recognized as a major foundation stone of the Romantic movement, which subsequently arose throughout the Western world.

With the appearance of this book in a number of translations, and of other works of similar nature, floodgates were opened, releasing a wealth of spiritual-cultural expressions in the field of the arts as a whole and in literature above all.

First among the host of Romantic writers active at this time was Johann Wolfgang von Goethe (1749–1832). His lyric poems, *Faust Part I*, *The Fairy Tale of the Green Snake and the Beautiful Lily*, and his translation of the *Songs of Selma* from Ossian into German show his deep connection with the Romantic movement. In Great Britain these writers included Lord Byron, Keats, Shelley, Wordsworth, Tennyson, and many others. In addition to their original contributions, these Romantics also made notable explorations into the folklore, fairy tales, mythology, and linguistics of a number of countries. For example in

1812, the first edition of the German *Fairy Tales* collected by the Brothers Grimm appeared. Shortly after came the *Eventyr*, the folk tales of Norway, gathered by Asbjornson and Moe; in Finland Elias Leinrot assembled folk songs and traditions, uniting them in the epic of the *Kalevala;* in Russia, Afanassieff produced his extraordinary collection of fairy tales from various parts of the Russian empire, during the time that Pushkin was writing his remarkable fairy tales, thus demonstrating the potential of Russian as a literary language, above all in his *Ruslan and Ludmilla.*

In the same period, a broad spectrum of Romantic prose and poetry was being produced by a widespread and divergent variety of American writers. In New England, the eastern and southern states as well as through-out the expanding midwest, this group included: Cooper, Emerson, Hawthorne, Longfellow, Lowell, Twain, Cabel, Bryant, Irving, Whitman, Harte, as well as such scholars as Schoolcraft, Prescott, and Bancroft, who found inspiration in the tradition of the Native Americans.

As the nineteenth century drew toward its close, what had been the Romantic movement metamorphosed into such groups as, among others, the Celtic revival movement (Lady Gregory, W. B. Yeats, Fiona Macleod), and the diversified artistic strivings of the pre-Raphaelites (John Ruskin, the Rossetties, William Morris, Burne-Jones, and others). In all of this, readers everywhere were gripped by the fascination of "the long ago and far away," as Tennyson once described Romanticism.

In our own time Rudolf Steiner (1861–1925) made a major contribution, gave a kind of golden key, which can help us understand such changes in the cultural life, as for example, that from Classicism to Romanticism, a transition which is basic to the theme of this present book. Such transitions—and there are many in the course of human history—involve the fact that the consciousness of humanity has changed radically and repeatedly throughout the ages. The human relation to the divine world above, to the world of nature around, and to the life within, has passed through many stages of development. In this connection, it is important that we recognize that in reality there never have been primitive peoples, but simply human beings who under varied conditions of life on earth have experienced themselves and the world around them in differing ways.

In most ancient times men felt themselves to be children of the divine, and lived in a dream of the beauties of a lost paradise. The mythologies, religious customs, domestic and social life of the various peoples reflect man's changing awareness of himself and his world. In course of time, he felt increasingly that it was his task to take possession of the earth, to subdue it to his will. Toward the fulfillment of this aim, he exerted his slowly emerging powers of independent thought, feeling, and action.

As man's physical senses became more powerful, enabling him to understand his environment through his intellectual thinking, his ancient dreamlike way of looking at the world slowly became dormant. Little by little, in the course of many centuries, those faculties appeared that were needed for modern abstract thinking. These were essential to the eventual development of our modern world of technology. In this sense what we usually call history is basically a reflection of the developing consciousness and unfolding capacities of man himself in the various epochs of his life on earth.

This process is reflected most vividly in the realm of the spiritual-cultural life, for it involves the eternal longing of the human being to rise above limited natural existence through transforming what is found in the material world, into revelations of the divine and immortal. This longing has expressed itself—consciously or unconsciously—in the work of all artists in all periods of history, reflecting to some degree their relationship to the world of spirit above them, to the world of nature around them, and to the life within them. An awareness of this evolving human consciousness as reflected in humanity's creative striving, is indispensable in face of the exhilarating opportunities and formidable obligations confronting the world today.

Toward an enhanced attainment of this awareness throughout history, world destiny has established certain earthly centers where spiritual-cultural achievements can come about under the wise guidance of spiritual leaders. This is clearly expressed in the words of Hilary in the opening scene of Rudolf Steiner's drama *The Guardian of the Threshold*. The original version of these words was significantly adapted for the opening of the Goetheanum at Dornach, Switzerland, on September 26, 1920. The following is the version read by Marie Steiner on that occasion:

> In that Spirit's name who reveals himself
> Through every striving living word here spoken
> I come to all those human beings in this hour
> Who henceforth will listen to the words
> Which here resound to human souls.
> The powers who guide our earthly progress
> Could not reveal themselves to fully awakened consciousness
> In most ancient times.
> For then it was as with children;
> Gradually the forces had to be matured and strengthened
> That ultimately were to bring about clear knowledge.
> So it was that all humanity
> Had slowly to unfold in course of time.
> At first the impulses of soul were weak
> But later showed themselves worthy
> To behold the spirit light from higher worlds.
>
> At earth's beginning higher powers chose
> From among those souls devoted to the spirit
> Those who were to serve as humanity's wise leaders.
> In places set aside for initiation striving,
> Mysteriously they called forth spirit forces,
> Sending knowledge into dimly conscious souls
> Who thereby filled themselves with inner sight.
> Later these wise leaders chose as pupils among humanity,
> Those who through trials of life
> Had become sufficiently mature to strive with zeal
> In clearest consciousness toward spirit knowledge.
> And when the pupils of those early teachers
> Learned to protect that spirit knowledge worthily,
> The higher guidance then withdrew,
> Thus allowing free souls to strive onward knowingly.

And in their turn these souls selected those
Who could succeed them in protecting the spirit treasure.
And so it continued through generations without number.
Thus to this day all centers of true knowledge
Descend directly from the highest
That can be found in spirit realms.

In earnest search we strive to find our truest spirit heritage,
Speaking of knowledge descending out of highest spirit realms.
It can reveal itself to those striving with clear sight
And putting their trust in it,
Thus fathoming the depths of their own souls.
To strive worthily toward the light of spirit knowledge
Our present time directs us in all earnestness.
Significant are the signs which world destiny
Shows clearly to the eye of spirit.

Rudolf Steiner, the author of these words, was a well-known Austrian educator and philosopher, who was deeply interested in cosmology, in earthly and planetary evolution, in ancient peoples, in social questions, and in furthering the cultural life through the arts. This was the fruit of his profound intuitive insight, his spiritual sensitivity, and his endless enthusiasm. Inspired by Goethe, notably by his natural scientific works, Steiner was a pioneer in the fullest and best sense of the word. His voice was that of one speaking amid the materialism of his time. His idealism, courage, and energy were truly Michaelic. All this united in enabling him to found Anthroposophy—the modern science of spirit. In his written works and nearly six thousand lectures, given over more than twenty-five years, he dealt with a wide range and variety of subjects, many from highly original points of view.

In Berlin on the afternoon of March 3, 1911, Rudolf Steiner gave an address in the official residence of the German chief of staff, General Helmuth von Moltke. The occasion included a performance of Felix Mendelssohn's Hebridean Overture, the Fingal's Cave music, followed by Rudolf Steiner's contribution in which he referred to James Macpherson's translation of *The Poems of Ossian*, to Fingal, and gave a vivid description of Fingal's Cave itself. So far as is known, Rudolf Steiner himself never visited Fingal's Cave on the isle of Staffa nor any of the western isles of Scotland, nor did he speak about Ossian or Fingal at any other time.

Careful study of the content of Rudolf Steiner's address has convinced the authors of this book, concerning the uniqueness and profound importance of his words spoken on March 3, 1911, and their relevance to life today. Therefore they have taken the thoughts expressed in Steiner's address as guiding motifs and have placed them at the opening of each of the chapters that follow. (The complete text of the address in its original German is given in vol. 127 of the *Rudolf Steiner Gesamtausgabe,* published by Rudolf Steiner Verlag, Dornach, Switzerland, pp. 118–25. The following translation into English has been newly prepared by the authors of this book.)

2. House concert for the benefit of the association of musicians and performing artists in Berlin, held in the official residence of the chief of the general staff, Helmuth von Moltke, on March 3, 1911. Rudolf Steiner, front row, right of center, between Her Excellency, Eliza von Moltke, on his right and Marie Steiner, on his left.

1

The Rediscovery
of Fingal's Cave

Through the tones and harmonies of this Hebridean Overture, we are led in spirit by Felix Mendelssohn to the shores of Scotland, and in our souls, we have thus followed a path, which during the course of human evolution, has been deeply influenced by the secrets of destiny. For from entirely different regions of the western hemisphere of our earth, as if through a destined current of migration, various peoples were once transplanted into the vicinity of that region, into which this music has now led us. And by this means, mysterious destinies unfold themselves to us, when we are told, both by what spiritual insight reveals, as well as through outer traces of history, what people experienced in most ancient times in this particular part of the earth.

A memory of the mysterious destinies of those people (inhabitants of the highlands and islands of western Scotland) arose again, as if newly awakened, when in 1772 Fingal's Cave, on the island of Staffa belonging to the Hebrides, was visited.

—Rudolf Steiner, March 3, 1911

Though untold millennia, its shores lashed by ocean storms and tides, the lonely isle of Staffa with its hidden caves and its powerful basaltic formations remained an almost forgotten evidence of "a structure architecturally formed entirely out of the spiritual world itself" (Rudolf Steiner).

However, it is not inconceivable that from century to century, individuals in their fragile coracles may have been carried to the shores of Staffa by the capricious restless movement of the waters surrounding the western islands of Scotland. Such infrequent visitors left little in the form of tangible remains. Nonetheless, one link with Staffa's ancient past and its connection with Gaelic mythology, appears to have remained alive in the consciousness of the islanders, some of whom connected the principal cave on Staffa with the folk memory of Fingal, the great initiate leader of an otherwise forgotten past.

One cannot fail to recognize that in our age of the modern consciousness soul, a clear contrast exists in how phenomena of nature such as Fingal's Cave are regarded, compared to the attitude of mind in which the ancient world of mythology is still alive and valid. To the latter, such phenomena were experienced out of profound, but not fully conscious, spiritual insight, while to the present-day mind these creations are largely seen as the direct result of the working of material forces through external nature. Indeed, in such a confrontation, two dissimilar worlds meet but do not mingle, thus confirming the validity of the observation to the effect that "matter is not what we see, but is *the way* we see creation."

One of the major results of the dawn of our modern age at the time of the Renaissance and during the years following, was man's ever-increasing interest in all details of the physical world, including even the most minute of them. Explorations of unknown seas, continents, deserts, jungles, vast mountain ranges, including their flora and fauna, formed the basis for an activity that continues to our present day. Among a host of explorers the names of two Englishmen stand out as having made important contributions in this striving to know ever more about the earth, its nature, and phenomena. These were Captain James Cook (1728–1779) and Sir Joseph Banks (1743–1820).

Their joint three-year expedition to the Pacific region and around the world (1768–1771) yielded a rich harvest of discoveries, especially in botanical and zoological specimens. (Botany Bay in Australia was named by Cook in honor of the notable contributions that Banks had made to their journey.) Prior to this, in 1776, Banks had carried out his first scientific expedition to Labrador and Newfoundland, bringing back invaluable specimens and drawings of plants and insects.

Following the journey to the southern hemisphere with Cook, Banks set out on an independent expedition to Iceland in 1772. Forced to interrupt his journey by adverse weather conditions, he took shelter in the Sound of Mull off the west coast of Scotland. While waiting for the winds to become moderate, he accepted an invitation from the local laird, a Mr. Macleane, who invited him to visit his estate. It was at this point that "by chance" destiny intervened, when Banks was introduced to yet another guest from England, a Mr. Leach. In the diary of Sir Joseph Banks (knighted in 1781, president of the Royal Society for forty-two years, an unprecedented length of tenure) the following vivid account portrays the overwhelming impression his visit to Staffa made on him and his companions:

> Aug. 12, 1772, in the Sound of Mull we came to anchor, on the Morven side, opposite to a gentleman's house called Drumnen. The owner of it, Mr. Macleane, having found out who we were, very cordially asked us ashore. We accepted his invitation and arrived at his house, where we met an English gentleman, Mr. Leach, who no sooner saw us, than he told us that about nine leagues from us was an island where he believed no one, even in the highlands, had been, on which were pillars like those of the Giant's Causeway. I cannot but express the obligations I have to this gentleman, for his very kind intention of informing me of this matchless curiosity, for I am informed that he pursued me in a boat for two miles, to acquaint me with what he had observed, but unfortunately for me, we outfailed his liberal intention. Later, when I lay in the Sound of Iona, two gentlemen from the isle of Mull, whose settlements were there, seemed to know nothing of this place, at least they never mentioned it as anything wonderful.
>
> I therefore resolved to proceed directly, especially as it was just in the way to Columb-Kill (the isle of Iona). Accordingly, having put up two days provisions and my little tent, we put off in the boat about one o'clock, for our intended voyage, having ordered the ship to wait for us in Tobirmore, a very fine harbor on the Mull side.
>
> At nine o'clock, after a tedious passage, having not had a breath of wind, we arrived under the direction of Mr. Macleans' son and Mr. Leach. It was too dark to see anything, so we carried our tent

and baggage near the only house on the island, and began to cook our supper, in order to be prepared for the earliest dawn, to enjoy what from the conversations of the gentlemen, we had now raised the highest expectations of.

The impatience which everyone felt to see the wonders we had heard so largely described, prevented our morning rest. Everyone was up and in motion before the break of day, and with the first light arrived at the southwest part of the island, the seat of the most remarkable pillars. We no sooner arrived than we were struck with a scene of magnificence, which exceeded our greatest expectations, though formed, as we thought on the most sanguine foundations. The whole of that end of the island is supported by ranges of natural pillars, mostly above fifty feet high, standing in natural colonnades, according as the bays or points of land formed themselves. Upon a firm basis of solid unformed rock, the stratum which reaches to the soil or surface of the island, varied in thickness as the island itself formed into hills or valleys, each hill, which hung over the columns below, forming an ample pediment. Some of these are above sixty feet in thickness from the base to the point formed by the sloping of the hill on each side, almost into the shape of those used in architecture.

Compared to this, what are the cathedrals or the palaces built by men! Mere models or playthings, imitations as diminutive as his works will always be when compared to those of nature. Where is now the boast of the architect! Regularity, the only part in which he fancied himself to exceed his mistress, nature, is here found in her possession, and here it has been for ages undescribed. Is this not the school where the art was originally studied, and what has been added to this by the whole Grecian school? A capital to ornament the column of nature, of which they could execute only a model, and for that very capital, they were obliged to a bush of Acanthus. How amply does nature repay those who study her wonderful works!

With our minds full of such reflections we proceeded along the shore, treading upon another Giant's Causeway, every stone being regularly formed into a certain number of sides and angles, until in a short time we arrived at the mouth of the cave, the most magnificent I suppose, that has ever been described by travelers.

The mind can hardly form an idea more magnificent than such a space, supported on each side by ranges of columns, and roofed by the bottoms of those which have been broken off in order to form it. Between the angles a yellow stalagmitic matter has exuded, which serves to define the angles precisely, and at the same time vary the color with a great deal of elegance. To render it still more agreeable, the whole is lighted from without, so that the furthest extremity is very plainly seen, and the air within being agitated by the flux and reflux of the tides, is perfectly dry and wholesome, free entirely from the damp vapors with which natural caverns in general abound.

We asked the name of it. Said our guide, the cave of Finn. What is Finn? said we. Finn MacCoul, whom James Macpherson, the translator of Ossian's works has called Fingal, said our guide. How fortunate that in this cave we should meet with the remembrance of that chief, whose existence, as well as that of the whole Epic poem is almost doubted in England!

Climax: Royalty Visits Fingal's Cave

ᑭᒃ It is now just over 150 years ago that on Thursday, August 19, 1847, Queen Victoria, Prince Albert, Charles Prince of Wales, and the princess royal, together with their entourage visited Staffa on their tour of the western isles of Scotland aboard the royal yacht. Queen Victoria records the following in her *Leaves from Our Journal of Our Life in the Highlands*:

At three o'clock we anchored close before Staffa and immediately got into the barge with Charles, the children, and the rest of our people, and rowed toward the cave. As we rounded the point, the wonderful basaltic formation came in sight. The appearance it presents is most extraordinary and when we turned the corner to go into the renowned Fingal's Cave, the effect was splendid, like a great entrance into a vaulted hall. It looked almost awful as we entered and the barge heaved up and down on the swell of the sea. It is very high, but not longer than 227 feet, and narrower than I expected, being only 40 ft wide. The sea is immensely deep in the cave. The rocks under water were of all colors—pink, blue and green—which had a most beautiful and varied effect. It was the first time the British standard with a Queen of Great Britain, and her husband and children had ever entered Fingal's Cave and the men gave three cheers, which sounded very impressive there. We backed out and then went on a little further to look at the other caves and at the point called The Herdsman. The swell was beginning to get up and perhaps an hour later we could not have gone in.

We returned to the yacht, but Albert and Charles landed again at Staffa. They returned in three quarters of an hour and we then went on to Iona. Here Albert and Charles landed and were absent for an hour. I and the ladies sketched. We saw from the yacht the ruins of the old cathedral of St. Oran. When Albert and Charles returned, they said the ruins were very curious. There had been two monasteries there, and fine old crosses and tombs of ancient kings were still to be seen. I must see it some other time. On Albert's return we went on again and reached Tobermory at nine. The place was all illuminated.

The publication and wide interest in Sir Joseph Bank's account of his visit to Staffa and Fingal's Cave, as well as the appearance in London of James Macpherson's *Poems of Ossian* in 1762, attracted many travelers from both Britain and the continent, already during the closing years of the eighteenth century. In the opening decades of the nineteenth century, articles appeared such as this one from *Lizar's Scottish Tourist*, a guide to the picturesque scenery and antiquities of Scotland, printed in Edinburgh :

Staffa is situated about eight miles from the coast of Mull and six miles south-west from Ulva. The island is of an irregular figure and nearly two miles in circumference, presenting a sort of table land bounded by cliffs varying in height and broken into numerous recesses and promontories. The greatest elevation is 144 feet, on the southwestern side. Its surface is covered with a rich verdure and in summer is pastured by black cattle. There is now neither a house nor a shepherd's hut upon the island.

The eastern coast of Staffa may almost always be safely approached. The usual and most frequented landing-place is on that side of the island. Here commence those magnificent columns which form the great attraction of this celebrated spot. The precipitous face of Staffa extends from the Clamshell Cave on the southeast to the Cormorant's or McKinnon's Cave on the south-west side. The highest point of this face lies between Fingal's Cave and the Boat-Cave and is 112 feet from high water mark.

On rounding the south-east promontory the exterior of Fingal's Cave presents itself to the view. The original Gaelic name is Uaimh Binn (the musical cave), a name derived from the echo of the waves. The wonders of this place cannot be thoroughly seen unless it be entered in a boat, by which it is accessible generally in all states of tide. The entrance to the cave, which is about sixty feet high and forty-two feet wide, resembles a Gothic arch. The stupendous columns that bound the interior sides of the cave are perpendicular, and being frequently broken and grouped in a variety of ways, a very picturesque effect is produced. The roof in some places is formed of rock and in others of the broken ends of pillars, from the interstices of which have exuded stalactites, producing a variety of beautiful tints, which have a fine effect, the whole resembling mosaic work. As the tide never ebbs out entirely, the only floor of this cave is the beautiful green sea, reflecting from its bosom those tints which vary and harmonize with the darker hues of the rock. The appearance of Fingal's Cave strongly excites the wonder and admiration of visitors, who are overpowered by the magnificence of the scene. The broken range of columns, forming the exterior causeway already noted, is continued on each side within the cave. This want of uniformity in the pavement becomes far more regular on the eastern side and admits of access nearly to the furthest extremity.

The finest views are obtained on the right of the entrance, from the end of the causeway at about low water, which is the most favorable period for viewing the beauties of the cave, and if possible, with the morning sun. From this position the front presents a solid mass of great breadth of surface. The entrance of the cave forms, as it were, a frame which gives relief to the view, while the eye explores the vast recess.

The variety and grandeur of the scenery of Staffa and particularly Fingal's Cave is such that upon repeated visits, it continues to rise in the estimation of all who are capable of relishing such stupendous operations of nature.

One of the most notable architects to visit Staffa over the years was Karl Friedrich Schinkel (1781–1841), eminent German architect, painter, and professor, active largely in Berlin University. Following his visit in 1826, two fellow countrymen of his arrived there in August 1829. These were Karl Klingemann, an intimate friend of the Mendelssohn family, who at this time accompanied the twenty-year-old Felix (1809–1847) on a tour of the Scottish Hebrides. In a letter written by Mendelssohn to his family, from Britain, he described the impression Scotland made on him: "The country is large and wide, thickly overgrown and forested, with ample streams tumbling under bridges from all directions, little corn, much heather, gorges, passes, crossroads, beautiful green and deep blue water everywhere, but everything is solemn, dark and rather lonely—How shall I describe it?"

On August seventh, the two young men set out from Oban on the newly introduced paddle steamer service sailing around Mull, stopping at Iona and Staffa. In his journal, Klingemann describes in a warm human manner, an incident that occurred on their journey:

There sat placidly by the steam engine, warming herself in the cold wind, a woman of two and eighty. She wanted to see Staffa before her end. Staffa, with its strange basaltic pillars and caverns is in all the picture books. We were put out in boats and lifted up by the hissing sea, up the pillar stumps to the celebrated Fingal's Cave. A greener roar of waves surely never rushed into a stranger cavern, its many pillars making it look like the inside of an immense organ, black and resounding, and absolutely without purpose, and quite alone, the wide gray sea within and without. There the old woman scrambled about laboriously, close to the water. She wanted to see the cave of Staffa before her end and she saw it. We then safely returned in the little boat to our steamer.

This visit to Staffa resulted, as all the world knows, in Mendelssohn's finding inspiration that same evening, from the sight and sound of the rising and falling of the Atlantic swell echoed within Fingal's Cave, to write what ultimately appeared as his Hebridean Overture (Fingal's Cave). It is revelatory to turn to the chronology of the composition, which underwent extensive revisions and changes of title between 1829 and 1835, clearly showing a progression from the general geographical location of the Hebrides to the cave on Staffa. Mendelssohn began with *Die Hebriden* (the Hebrides) in 1830, but then turned to *Die einsame Insel* (The Lonely Island) also in 1830. Two years later in 1832 it was titled *The Isles of Fingal* for the first English performance, and finally at Rome the work was published in 1835 as *Fingalshöhle* (Fingal's Cave), thereby gradually defining the scope of the overture as specifically concerned with Fingal's Cave.

In his composition, Mendelssohn indeed describes most vividly the impact that Fingal's Cave made upon him, painting these impressions in his own medium of subtle musical tones, similar to a painter's use of his palette of colors. The work is based upon the movement of the sea, as an element that is in perpetual change, yet ever remains the same. The entire thematic material is grounded upon a brief motif, which though continually varied, nevertheless is present thoughout the whole composition in an always recognizable form.

During the brief eleven minutes required to perform the overture, the listener is swept into an experience of swirling, relentless, undulating, never-ending movement characteristic of the restlessness of the tides and currents of the sea. This turbulence is interspersed and balanced by tender melodic interludes, at times portrayed by the gentle watery tones of the woodwinds. To the listener, such moments are like the gentle rays of the passing sunlight, as it breaks through the often present clouds and shimmers on the momentarily calm surface of the water.

Just as the music paints a living portrait of Fingal's Cave, in the same way it is clear that it forms a living link to the atmosphere of *The*

Poems of Ossian themselves. The interplay between the strong martial tones of the percussions and brasses, reminiscent of the heroic battle passages in the poems, stands in marked contrast to the lyric episodes occurring in the music, reminding one of the gentleness and pathos, especially as expressed in Ossian's heroines. Both the words of the poems and the tones of the music bear the soulful impress of the twilight mood, the characteristic "backward glance" of the Gael. All of this reflects the mood of autumn, of "joy in grief," of the noble sentimentality of the Ossianic heroes. As the overture draws to its close, three times the motif of the ever-restless sea gently echoes, the whole work concluding on a lonely high note of the oboe. This final moment suggests a fleeting glimpse of a vanishing, heroic, Ossianic world, fading into obscurity just as quietly and unostentatiously as it began.

In similar manner, at the conclusion of *The Songs of Selma*, the final book of *The Poems of Ossian*, all the heroes have withdrawn into the spiritual world and are no longer visible to us, but like the last words of Goethe's *Chorus Mysticus* in his *Faust, Part 11*, they rise higher and higher into a world where our earthborn sense can no longer follow them, and a fading dream alone is left to us.

As he makes fully clear in his address of March 3, 1911, Rudolf Steiner experienced in Ossian's poems the fruit of the working of destiny (*Schicksal/Karma,* a word appearing a total of eight times in Steiner's text) among men in an earlier period in the unfolding life of the Western world. Steiner clearly indicated that destiny is expressed most profoundly in the Ossianic poems themselves, primarily through their "rhythms and sounds," as well as in the effect upon the reader, above all on anyone opening his inner life to their influence. Steiner opens and closes his 1911 address with a direct reference to the "tones and harmonies" (Klänge) of Mendelssohn's Hebridean Overture, thereby establishing a clear link between the archetypal formative force physically manifest in Fingal's Cave on the one hand, and the spiritual essence of *The Poems of Ossian* on the other.

En route to Staffa, Mendelssohn had been a guest at Abbottsford, the home of Sir Walter Scott. During the following summer, 1830, Joseph Mallord William Turner (1775–1851), probably Britain's most famous landscape painter, in response to a request from Scott to make twenty-four drawings as illustrations for Scott's new work *The Lord of the Isles*, had also visited Abbottsford and made many sketches in the neighborhood. It was then, at the suggestion of Scott who had visited Staffa previously, that Turner, traveling on the steamer the *Maid of Morven*, went to Staffa and while there made an impressionistic sketch of the view from inside Fingal's Cave looking out over the sea toward Iona. Later Turner created a major oil painting, *Staffa, Fingal's Cave*, which was shown in the Royal Academy Exhibition, London, in 1832.

During these same years a number of other British artists were inspired by the romantic qualities of *The Poems of Ossian* and by the stupendous drama of Fingal's Cave itself. Among these were William Daniell (1769–1837) with his aquatint engravings for *A Voyage Round Great Britain*, 1825, and Thomas Pennant's many illustrations of Staffa contained in his celebrated *A Tour in Scotland and Voyage to the Hebrides*, 1790.

In addition to Sir Walter Scott, numerous poets and writers were inspired by visits to Fingal's Cave and in prose and verse expressed their enthusiasm for this natural wonder. These included William Wordsworth, Alfred Lord Tennyson, Jules Verne, Robert Louis Stevenson, and John Keats, the latter writing this prose description based on his mythological imagination:

> Suppose now that giants who came down to the daughters of men had taken a whole mass of these columns, and bound them together like bunches of matches, and then with immense axes had made a cavern in the body of these columns. Such is Fingal's Cave, except that the sea has done the work of excavating and is continually dashing there. The color of the columns is a sort of black, with a lurking gloom of purple therein. For solemnity and grandeur it far surpasses the finest cathedral.

In 1896, for the centenary edition of *The Poems of Ossian*, William Sharp, better known under the pseudonym Fiona Macleod (1856–1905), as one of the foremost figures in the Celtic revival movement, was accorded the honor of editing and introducing this outstanding volume. In a collection of his own poems he wrote thus about Staffa:

The Caves of Staffa

The green Atlantic seas wash past,
The mighty pillars of basalt;
A vast sea-echo through the vault
Swells like a captive thunder-blast;
The wind, fierce showers of spray doth sweep
Through the cave's gulf, and loud the deep.
Resistless billows in their course
Thunder within in tumult hoarse.

Among the many Americans who visited Fingal's Cave was Brett Harte (1839–1902), the well-known novelist and poet. While acting as U.S. Consul in Glasgow he visited Staffa, saying it was the only sight in Europe that quite fulfilled his expectations. The celebrated theater critic and author, William Winter, friend of Longfellow and Emerson, recalled in these words the powerful impression Fingal's Cave made on him: "it is a solemn and awful place, and you behold it without words and leave it in silence, but your backward look remains long fixed upon it, and its living picture of gloom and glory will never fade out of your mind."

Mary Anderson, the celebrated American actress, wrote in one of her letters: "I shall never forget my first visit to Staffa on the Grenadier. It was a beautiful summer day. As the small boat entered Fingal's Cave I was quite breathless at seeing such loveliness; there is nothing else like it in the world. Such an array of rich colors as the sunlight sparkled on the sea and on the lichened rock of this pillared cavern, I never saw before and have never seen since. It is a beautiful fairyland and seems almost too beautiful for reality. It makes one feel as if one is having a glorious dream. In my memory and in my dreams, when they are especially good ones, this wonderful scene lives as clearly as when I first viewed it."

Two contemporary Scottish writers visited Fingal's Cave and described their impressions. The journalist William Power (1874–1951) wrote: "Fingal's Cave is the unique marvel of Scotland, as Stonehenge is of England." Neil Gunn (1891–1973), one of Scotland's greatest novelists, in his *Off in a Boat*, 1937, said: "Usually the showcases of a country are disappointing, but I must say Staffa was arresting. We had never seen anything like its pillared rock formation, for at first glance it struck in us an incredulous note, as if the southern rock face had been artificially carved into high relief columns and then the whole erection given a slight tilt. It certainly did not look like a piece of work by haphazard nature. . . . Staffa comes upon one with an air of surprise and wonder, like a work of genius in a picture frame. We could hear the modulated note of the booming waves, and remembered the old Gaelic name Uaimh Binn, the melodious cavern."

June 9, 1997, marked the 1400th anniversary of the death of St. Columba on Iona in 597. Just one hundred years earlier, on June 10, 1897, a memorable event took place in Fingal's Cave. On the previous day, a group of eminent Scottish Divines had celebrated a special commemorative service in the ruins of the Abbey Church on Iona, the first public worship to be held there for over three hundred years.

The next day, a gathering of about three hundred persons, accompanied by these same Scottish church leaders, gathered in Fingal's Cave on Staffa. Moved by the majestic surrounding and spiritual atmosphere of the place, they spontaneously gave expression to the inspiration of that moment by singing the 103rd Psalm set to the traditional tune of Coleshill:

> O thou my soul bless God the lord;
> And all that in me is,
> Be stirred, his holy name
> To magnify and bless.
>
> Bless O my soul, the Lord thy God,
> And not forgetful be
> Of all his gracious benefits
> He hath bestowed on thee.
>
> All thine iniquities who doth
> Most graciously forgive;

Who thy diseases all and pains
Doth hear, and thee relieve.

Who doth redeem thy life, that thou
To death mayst not go down;
Who thee with loving kindness doth
And tender mercies crown.

Who with abundance of good things
Doth satisfy thy mouth;
So that even as the eagle's age,
Renewed is thy youth.

In September 1894, the British public was officially permitted to send pictorial postcards through the mail system of the country for the first time. The result was that almost overnight a host of photographic reproductions and artistic renditions of natural and man-made places of interest appeared everywhere. One of the most popular subjects soon proved to be a wide selection of views of the Hebridean isle of Staffa, its caves, its visitors, and the boats that brought them to the island. Among the leading sources in supplying this demand were the firms of Valentines of Dundee, Wilsons of Aberdeen, and Wrench of London. Quick to recognize the commercial value of such illustrative material was David MacBrayne, Ltd., shipping company of Glasgow, who for a number of years from 1900 onward used a drawing of Fingal's Cave on their official letterhead.

It was about the turn of the century that the firm of Train and McIntyre, Ltd., Distillers of Glasgow, placed on the market a Scottish whiskey labeled with the unique name of "Dew of the Western Isles," printed across a romanticized drawing of Fingal's Cave. It was not long before a number of artists turned their skill toward depicting various views of Staffa in watercolor and "Oilette" techniques. Among these were J. W. Carey, who early in the century painted the "Royal Route Series" for MacBraynes and Tom Gilfillan's watercolor series in the 1930s.

Although there has never been the possibility of keeping any accurate record of the innumerable visitors to Staffa following its rediscovery in 1772, the island having remained practically uninhabited during these years, it is clear that Staffa has attracted countless visitors from many lands during the intervening more that two hundred years. In recent times it has become easier for travelers to land on Staffa, due to the construction of a new landing stage at Clamshell Cave in 1991, and to regular daily scheduled visits during May through September, "weather permitting," from both Iona and the island of Ulva, lying off the coast of Mull.

Since the rediscovery of Staffa by Sir Joseph Banks in 1772, probably no visitor has shown more enthusiasm, appreciation, and genuine love for the island and its natural wonders than did the late Baron Richard Austin Butler (1902–1980). Following the second world war, it is said that scarcely a year passed when he did not visit Staffa at least once, continuing this practice until shortly before his death. Considered by many to have been "one of the finest prime ministers Britain never had," he devoted his entire life to serving the British people in a number of important and outstanding capacities. His popularity, ability, and good humor are reflected in his widely read autobiography *The Art of the Possible*.

In 1986, the island of Staffa was given to the National Trust of Scotland through the generosity of Mr. John Elliot, Jr., of New York, former chairman of Ogilvy and Mather, as a unique way of honoring the sixtieth birthday of his wife Elly. She in turn has meanwhile been declared by the trust as steward of Staffa for her lifetime.

Now all who value the seclusion and awesome beauty of Staffa need not fear for its future, since the National Trust of Scotland provides assurance that the island, including Fingal's Cave, a masterpiece "architecturally formed entirely out of the spiritual world itself," will remain unchanged through all future times.

3. The discoverer:
Sir Joseph Banks,
Bart. (1743-1820).

4. Eighteenth-century sketch map showing Staffa surrounded by islands of the Inner Hebrides off western Scotland.

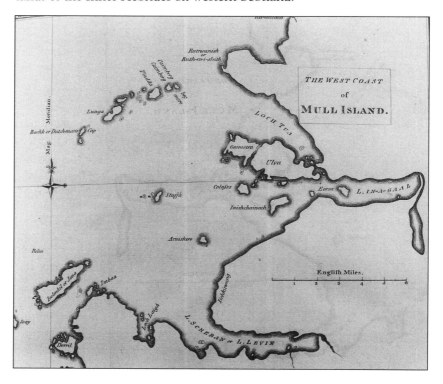

5. Queen Victoria and Prince Albert welcomed at Edinburgh, en route to their visit to the Hebrides. Arthur's Seat is in the background.

6. The Royal Barge entering Fingal's Cave, August 19, 1847.

7. Early nineteenth-century engraving: entrance to Fingal's Cave seen from causeway at the southeast.

8. Looking into Fingal's Cave: nineteenth-century artistic impression.

9. LEFT: Felix Mendelssohn (1809-1847), sketch Leipzig, 1840.

10. RIGHT: Karl Klingemann, Mendelssohn's companion on his Scottish tour, 1829.

11. Opening bars of *Hebridean Overture (Fingal's Cave)*. Facsimile in Mendelssohn's hand, written the evening following his visit to Staffa.

12. View from interior of Fingal's Cave. Sketch by J. M. W. Turner, 1830.

13. *Staffa: Fingal's Cave*, oil painting by J. M. W. Turner, 1832.

14. Sketch of J. M. W. Turner, made at about the time of his visit to Staffa in 1830.

15. Postcard ca, 1882, by Valentine's of Dundee, Landing Place, Fingal's Cave.

16. Postcard ca. 1889, by Valentine's of Dundee, at the Clamshell Cave.

17. Postcard ca. 1889, by Valentine's of Dundee, Staffa from the sea.

18. Postcard ca. 1896, by J. B. White, Ltd., Dundee, west side of Staffa.

19. Highland Whiskey label, ca. 1900, showing Fingal's Cave.

20. Postcard ca. 1910—Oilette view of Fingal's Cave, Staffa.

21. Postcard ca. 1930—Approaching Staffa, watercolor view by Tom Gilfillan.

22. Postcard ca. 1930—Diorama, Staffa, by B. Matthews, Ltd.

23. Postcard ca. 1947-1954, by Valentine's of Dundee, The Herdsman, Staffa.

THE HERDSMAN, ISLE OF STAFFA   B 715

24. Postcard ca. 1947-1954, by Valentine's of Dundee, Fingal's Cave.

25. Drawing: interior of Fingal's Cave, Staffa.

2

Earthly Settings for
Spiritual Enlightenment

What happened in the vicinity of the Hebrides, in Ireland and Scotland, in ancient Erin, on the neighboring islands between Ireland and Scotland, as well as the northern part of Scotland itself? It is there we must seek for the kernel of those peoples of Celtic origin, who had most of all preserved the ancient Atlantian clairvoyance in its fullest purity. The others who had wandered more to the East, having developed further, no longer kept their earlier connection with the ancient gods. In contrast, the Celtic peoples preserved for themselves the possibility of experiencing the old clairvoyance and therefore they were fully immersed in the element of individuality. These people were guided to this particular part of the earth, as if for a special mission. Here Fingal's Cave, a structure which had been architecturally formed entirely out of the spiritual world, stood before them, mirroring their own musical inner depths.

—*Rudolf Steiner, March 3, 1911*

 A deeper study of the spiritual backgrounds of earthly history shows that the migrations of peoples in the long course of human life on earth invariably were guided by leading personalities prepared for this task. Consideration of the various historical epochs clearly indicates that such figures as the Sumerian priest-kings, the pharaohs, Moses, Buddha, Aristotle, Alexander, and others experienced the same physical influences of time and place as did all their contemporaries. Yet they nevertheless were able to transform the consciousness, the worldview, and the destinies of their own peoples, and that of whole regions of the earth as well.

From the ancient myths and traditions, which tell of spiritual leaders and heroes of primeval days, one learns of events that took place in earlier times. One is thus transported into happenings of mythical and heavenly history, when it was possible for beings of a higher order to guide the deeds and development of earthly humans. Hence the spiritual striving of all times has been directed toward achieving harmony between cosmos, earth, and humanity as a whole.

The initiate leader Fingal, generally known as Finn in Irish mythology, along with his followers, formed the kernel of those people of Celtic origin, who most of all preserved the ancient spiritual insight in fullest purity. It is essential to recognize that when a name like Fingal is mentioned in old traditions, one is not referring only to a single person, but that for the most part this name designates a particular spiritual stream, flowing through a multitude of generations, from antiquity to later times. In like manner Manes, Melchisedek, Abraham, Zarathustra, King Arthur, and others can be considered to be mystery names, denoting specific spiritual currents that often span centuries, rather than being limited to the lifetime of a single individual.

The fact that biblical, classical, and medieval writers were so often preoccupied with identifying family relationships among the individualities named in their writings, expresses the great emphasis they placed on blood ties, which for them formed the basis of human community. Therefore, what may be called "Communities of the Blood" arose, essentially derived from corporeal physical relationships existing between members of the group. These relationships often involved mortal combat, fierce battles, and much bloodshed between the various groups or clans, set against a background of tempestuous nature. Guidance was frequently sought from the spirits of those who had already died in battle, and who in the course of time were honored as heroes and even demigods, thus ultimately forming a basis for what is commonly referred to as ancestor worship.

Thus, out of that region of northwestern Europe inhabited by the Celtic peoples, arose a great wealth of myths, epics, and sagas. Among these were the Irish Tain, the Eddas of Iceland, the Heimskringla Saga from Scandinavia, the Dream Song of Olaf Åsteson from Telemark in Norway, the Welsh Mabinogion, the Arthurian traditions of Britain, the Epic of Raud and his sons, the Frithiof Saga of Sweden, and the Saga of the Ring of the Niebelungs from Germany and Scandinavia.

These and many similar works, handed down from mouth to ear, and later preserved in written form, are a part of the rich spiritual heritage reflecting "the full purity of the ancient clairvoyance." They can remind one of the guidance and inspiration emanating from the stream of Fingal, that hero who once upon a time guided his people out of their primeval homeland into another part of the earth, where they were destined to lay the foundations of a future epoch for humanity.

When one reads *The Poems of Ossian*, one cannot but be impressed by his profound poetic descriptions of the life of Nature. Not only the sea, rivers, streams, weather, seasons, winds, and mountains form the physical setting for the events described in his epics, but violent tempests, and catastrophic natural phenomena frequently enwrap and surround all that happens, giving the events a powerful and distinctive quality.

Nearer to our own time Shakespeare has given us echoes of this earlier Celtic mood in the storm scene in King Lear, the shipwreck in the Tempest, and the heath scene with the witches in the opening of Macbeth. In the Fingal epic, one finds a variety of allusions to the world of Nature. In Book IV, Ossian describes the deceased Malvina, daughter of the hero Toscar, and in the gathering darkness, the battle taking place on the heath of Lena:

> Beside the murmur of Branno, thou didst often sit, O Maid! Thy white bosom rose frequently, like the down of the swan when slow she swims on the lake, and sidelong winds blow on her ruffled wing. Thou hast seen the sun retire, red and slow behind his cloud, night gathering round on the mountain, while the unfrequent blast roared in the narrow vales. At length the rain beats hard, thunder rolls in peels, lightning glances on the rocks! Spirits ride on beams

of fire! The strength of the mountain streams comes roaring down the hills. Such was the noise of battle!

In Book V, describing the death of Ryno, Fingal thus laments the loss of his youngest son:

> Calm was Ryno in the days of peace. He was like the rainbow of the shower seen far distant on the stream, when the sun is setting on Mora, when silence dwells on the hill of deer. Rest youngest of my sons, rest O Ryno on Lena. We too shall be no more. Warriors one day must fall.

Book VI concludes the Fingal epic, opening with the following decription of nature:

> The clouds of night come rolling down. Darkness rests on the steeps of Cromla. The stars of the north arise over the rolling of Erin's waves. They show their heads of fire, through the flying mist of heaven. A distant wind roars in the wood. Silent and dark is the plain of death.

Careful study of biography shows that in many instances *where* a person was born is of equal significance to *when* the birth took place. This also holds true in relation to certain locations on the earth, which throughout centuries, even millennia, have been recognized as places where a more intimate experience of the presence and effect of the working of spiritual beings has proved possible. Thus throughout the long history of mankind, we find in almost every part of the globe certain natural settings where a direct living relationship with the spiritual can come about. Hardly a region of the earth exists where holy mountains and islands, sacred wells, lakes, springs, rivers, and groves, as well as natural caves and grottos, cannot be found.

For the most part these holy places were originally dedicated to one or another planetary mystery teaching, or in later times to a Christian saint. Thus these particular settings were surrounded and impregnated with tradition, giving rise to a wealth of legends, myths, and sacred practices. It is not surprising, therefore, that in the world of Fingal and the Celts, as well as among all peoples of ancient times, a wealth of such places are mentioned and play a vital role in the unfolding of their epics and folklore.

Since the earliest dimly veiled times of prehistory, ascending a hill or mountain has always evoked in the human being a sense of being lifted up, accompanied by a degree of spiritual exhilaration, often not unmixed with a certain feeling of fear, awe, or reverence. Here we can recall John Ruskin's words: "to men of ancient times, mountains were worthy of reverence and of enjoyment, so long as they were far away." Thus it is clear that people did not climb "the high places" for sport or pleasure as is often the case today.

To call to mind the places and names of mountains famous in antiquity is in itself sufficient to remind one of the awe and wonder their image often inspired: Olympus, the home of the Greek gods, Meru, in central Asia, Ayers Rock, sacred to the aborigines of Australia, and Fujiyama ("that which remains") in Japan, object of reverent pilgrimages to this day. Turning to biblical history, one finds Mount Ararat, famous in the days of Noah, Sinai where Moses communed with God, Zion, site of Solomon's temple in Jerusalem, Mount Tabor, scene of the Transfiguration, as well as Mount Athos, still a center for eastern Christian worship.

However, more directly connected with the theme of this book, is Ireland's hill of Tara, in County Meath. Standing isolated in the gentle green landscape, Tara has played a central role in the long religious, political, and cultural history of the Irish people. To this day, on its summit six raths, or circular earth works, are still visible. Here was preserved the holy "Stone of Destiny" on which many Irish rulers were crowned. Until A.D. 560 Tara was famous as the central seat of druidism in Ireland, after which, through the deeds of St. Ruadan, it became a venerated center of Christianity.

Surrounded by the sea, the particular isolation of islands often evokes in their inhabitants experiences of protection, self-identity, loneliness, as well as strong qualities of inner self-reliance, courage, and resourcefulness. In the classic world, the poets sang of the wonders of the Hesperides, Dante describes the Purgatorio as located on an island, and Francis of Assisi regularly celebrated Michaelmas-Lent each year on the Isola Maggiore, in Lake Trasimeno. Familiar to all children are the islands of Robinson Crusoe as well as Swiss Family Robinson, memorable for many of the qualities mentioned above.

The Hebridean islands, greatly varying in size and character, are a well-known part of the setting for the Celtic world, their shores washed by the tempestuous waters of the north Atlantic. A number of these islands are regarded as holy places because of their association with the ancient heroes and events of Celtic mythology. Later their names became linked with the personalities of early Christian saints, for whom such isolated islands provided a setting for sacred activities and events, preserved in the legends concerning Saints Columba, Cuthbert, Kentigern, Brigit, and a host of others.

Probably the two most famous holy islands where Columban Christianity played a dominant role are Iona and Lindisfarne. The island of Hy, in the western Hebrides, now known as Iona, is inextricably associated with St. Columba and his companions. It has been a center of pilgrimage for more than fourteen centuries. Despite his vehement, outspoken opposition to *The Poems of Ossian*, as rendered by James Macpherson, the following words written by Dr. Samuel Johnson (1709–1784) during his tour of the Scottish highlands in 1773, may come as something of a surprise to those familiar with his otherwise critical attitude regarding the Celtic people and their world: "that man is little to be envied, whose patriotism would not gain force upon the plain of Marathon, or whose piety would not grow warmer among the ruins of Iona."

Lindisfarne, Iona's counterpart on the east coast of Northumberland, was the scene of the life and work of St. Cuthbert, whose remains are venerated in nearby Durham cathedral. Both these islands, with their centers of monastic Columban Christianity, were the sources from which groups of Celtic missionaries carried the gospel message throughout Britain and into what is now France, northern Italy, Switzerland, and parts of Austria and Hungary.

Selje, an island off the west coast of Norway associated with the touching story of the life of the Irish St. Sunniva; Skellig Michael, the rugged and precipitous crag, the summit of a submerged volcano lying fourteen miles off the southwest coast of Ireland, long a harsh setting for Irish penitent monks; and the isle of Staffa, in the Inner Hebrides off the west coast of Scotland, famous for its unique basaltic caves, are three further outstanding examples of sacred islands where Columban Christianity was fostered.

Wherever pure crystalline water flows, particularly when it rises from deep beneath the surface of the ground, the blessings of the earth goddess have long been regarded as manifest. This applies especially to the beneficient qualities long associated with what came to be regarded as sacred springs, pools, wells, lakes, and rivers. Early Christian churches and cathedrals were often built over pre-Christian wells and springs preserved in their crypt foundations. Thus the inclusion of the water or lunar element balanced the solar element, which was manifested in the cultic activities carried out in the building itself. From earliest times associated with the religious festivals of the Druids, the hill of Chartres has been the site of a sacred well, which can still be seen in the crypt of this outstanding Gothic cathedral located in northern France. Indeed it can be said that there is scarcely a structure created for religious observances that does not include the element of water in its environs. In the construction of temple precincts in the pre-Christian world, sacred pools were almost always to be found—the Temple of Karnac in Egypt, the Castalian spring at Delphi, the water clocks and hanging gardens of the Babylonians, the holy wells and pools of the Mayan and Aztec civilizations, the reflecting pools of oriental temples, such as that of the Taj Mahal, the pool of Siloam in Jerusalem.

Ever-memorable is the description that Tennyson gives of Sir Bedivere's return of King Arthur's sword Excalibur to the embrace of the enchanted depths of the sacred lake:

> So flashed and fell the brand Excalibur,
> But ere he dipt the surface, rose an arm
> Clothed in white samite, mystic, wonderful,
> And caught him by the hilt, and brandished him
> Three times, and drew him under in the mere.
> —*Idylls of the King, the Passing of Arthur*

At one time or another in the course of man's experience in various parts of the earth, rivers have assumed a profoundly spiritual quality for him, aside from their role in his daily life. Among these one can recall: the Ganges, the Nile, the Letha and the Acheron in Dante's *Divine Comedy*, the Styx in Greek mythology, the river Jordan in the Holy Land, and the ever-flowing of River of Life pictured in the Apocalypse of St. John.

When in 1990, an ancient shamaness living in a remote village in the Altai Mountains of northwestern Mongolia, was asked what was the best advice she could give to the younger generation of today, she replied without hesitation: "I would tell them; respect nature which is all around you. Look after the rivers and the streams because they supply the water which you drink. Look after the sky and the air which gives you heat, and care for the land because it feeds you." These wise and timely words make clear that the fundamental relationship between humans and the world of nature remains timeless and inviolate in the essential teachings of Buddhism as in other major religious disciplines.

The Celtic world was a region where sacred springs, wells, and groves abounded. Of the latter, two types of trees were particularly revered, the oak and the birch. As the tree connected with the qualities of Mars, strength, endurance, ruggedness of appearance, the oak stands in marked contrast to the gentle Venus qualities of the graceful birch, with the latter's tender, shimmering leaves, and silvery bark. Oak groves were particularly sacred to the Druids, who at certain seasons of the year cut the healing mistletoe from its branches, and in whose shadows the Druids held their philosophical discussions and taught their pupils. The gentle birch groves formed the setting for the gatherings of the Bards, who in their music recalled the deeds of heroes, the joys and sorrows of life, and celebrated the changing moods and seasons of the year.

On a clear day, from the highest point on the isle of Iona, one hundred meters above sea level, the summit of Dun I provides the visitor with an extraordinarily impressive panorama extending in all directions. To the northwest, beginning with the distant isles of Tiree and Coll, the eye beholds a vista of Rhum, Skye, with its towering Cullin massif, Staffa set against a background of the isle of Mull, the latter appearing against the mainland of Ardnamurchan. Turning farther to the east, the mountains of Argyll rise in the distance, while in the south the Paps of Jura and Islay complete the sequence of this most remarkable panorama. To the southwest no land is seen as one gazes across the expanses of the gray north Atlantic, beyond which lies North America, some three thousand miles distant.

Nestling between two huge boulders, at the verge of the steep northern face of Dun I, the crystal-clear waters of the Well of Eternal Youth mirror the starry sky at night and the rays of the sun by day. This is one of the oldest sacred wells in the Hebridean world and is named for St. Bride or Bridget. Long venerated as the "Mary of the Gael," one of the best-known popular legends concerning her role as the Foster-Mother of Christ describes the source of this tradition:

> The island of Iona lies in the western seas; and whoever has felt the breath of the wind and the kiss of the light above those lonely hills, knows that it is a holy place. For these shores were the haunt of St. Bride, the Foster-Mother of the King of the World.
>
> Dughall, Prince of Ireland, was driven from his native land. It was said that he had married a maiden against his father's will and that the child Bridget was his; but now it is known that no mortal father could claim that babe. The King was wroth and believed ill of his son, so Dughall and Bridget were placed in a tiny boat and set afloat on the wild waves. Surely no power could bring their frail craft to land. The clouds gathered and the wind rose. Lightning flashed across the dark sky. Dughall held the babe in his arms so that they should die together. But suddenly it seemed as though sunlight pierced the clouds and there in the glory of golden light shone a child with a face so gentle and mild that Dughall bowed his head. The child stretched forth his hands and lo! the wind sank and the waves were stilled. It seemed then to Dughall that the waters murmured, "O King of the Elements, we are thy servants and thy command shall be obeyed."
>
> A light breeze caught the frail boat and carried it gently through the waves to a quiet cove. Then the little maid who had not yet

stood or walked, stepped onto the beach and spoke words which Dughall did not understand.

"I am but a little child, yet these arms shall enfold the Lord of the World. The King of the Elements himself shall rest on my heart."

A white-robed priest came down to welcome the wanderers. He told them that they had been guided to the holy island of Iona where every dawn the sacred fire was kindled to greet the rising sun. From day to day the priests kept watch for they said that soon on earth a holy child was to be born who would be King of the Elements, and they would surely see the signs of his approach.

For many years, Dughall and Bridget lived on the island and the priests taught the young maid their holy lore. They welcomed her where no unhallowed foot might tread and she stood with them before the altar to greet the morning light.

It was Bridget's birthday and the island slumbered in the warm spring light. Robed in white she wandered over the hill to a place she loved to sit and dream. There between the rowan trees lay the mountain pool known as the Fountain of Youth. The trees were green with their first leaves and the waters reflected the ever changing light of sun and cloud. Bridget leaned over to drink the cool water and gazed into the still depths. But as she gazed she saw in wonder that behind the image of her own form there gleamed, not the wide blue sky and the passing clouds, but a beautiful woman standing with arms outspread as though in blessing. Above her the trees were no longer green as in early spring but they twined their branches to form a crown, bright with scarlet berries. The woman's gown was redder than the rowans and her outspread robe, shining with stars, a deeper blue than the midday sky. Bridget turned to see who stood behind her but no one was there, she was alone under the wide heavens.

Then a longing rose in her heart to seek this beautiful stranger but she did not know what path to follow.

A white thrush began to sing among the rowan trees and a dove flew down before her as though it wished to guide her on her way. Bridget followed until twilight spread its wings over the earth and from far away a golden star shed its guiding ray. Onward through mist and cloud, through water and light lay the path of Bridget, and when storms swept over the ocean, it seemed as though helping hands held her aloft and when the way led her through desert wastes, unseen powers nourished and supported her.

At last she found herself in a strange land where the trees were unknown to her and where the people spoke a foreign tongue. The earth was dry and hard as though with drought, the plants had withered and died, and the animals drooped for lack of water. Ahead of her lay a little village and among the houses clustering together on the mountain slope she saw a white inn. As she drew near, the landlord came to meet her and she saw that he was none other than her foster-father Dughall.

He showed no surprise but he said, "Guard my inn until my return. I go to seek for water from the Mount of Olives for there has been no rain and all the springs are dry. Promise me that you will admit no more guests for the inn is full and there is barely a morsel of food or a drop of ale left in the house."

Bridget took charge of the inn and for three days no rain fell and no drop of moisture came to bless the ground. The ale was almost gone and the water barrel was empty when on the third day she heard a knock on the door. Outside there stood an old man, bent with age, leading a donkey, and on its back was seated a beautiful woman.

"Pray give us shelter for the night," said the old man, "we have traveled far and Mary, my wife, is weary."

"The landlord has given me orders that no more guests be brought to the inn," said Bridget "for it is already crowded and there is no drink to spare."

She gazed at the woman sitting upon the ass and when she saw those deep dark eyes, memory stirred in her heart.

"O Bridget, do you not remember me?" asked the woman. "Who was it that gazed into your eyes by the mountain pool? Look into your heart and remember."

"It was you who stood beside me at the mountain pool," said Bridget, "and your mantle of stars embraced the whole wide world.

I may not admit you to the inn, but there is a stable which will shelter you from the cold and where you may rest, and I will bring you whatever food is left."

Bridget led the old man and his wife to the stable and brought them bread and ale. Yet when she returned to the inn she saw that the loaf of bread was untouched and the flagon of ale was full.

Late at night, Dughall returned from the Mount of Olives with his cruse full of water. Bridget began to tell him of the strange travelers but he cried to her to be silent and listen. There could be heard the sound of quiet rain falling upon the earth, yet above the sky was blue and cloudless.

"There is an old saying," said Dughall, "that when after long drought the rain falls from a cloudless heaven, the Lord of all the World will come to earth. Let us seek these strange travelers."

Bridget and her foster-father softly opened the door of the stable. So bright was the light shining through the dark abode that it seemed as though the sun himself had come to dwell therein. Between the ox and the ass sat the young mother with her child upon her knee, and Joseph kneeled before them in wonder and in love.

"Who is this child?" Dughall whispered in awe.

"The Prince of Peace." said Joseph.

Mary held out the little one to Bridget. "Bride, my sister, this night you shall be His nurse that I may sleep."

The maiden took the child and folding Him in her mantle, lulled Him on her heart until He slept.

Far away in Iona the Arch Druid Cathal was dying. But e'er he closed his eyes there dawned upon them the vision of Bride with the King of the Elements sleeping on her breast and he smiled for joy that this sight had been granted him before his death.

In the morning Mary took the child once more, and bending over Bride she kissed her softly with the words.

"From now through all eternity you shall be known as my sister, the foster-mother of the Holy Child."

Bride fell into a deep slumber and when she awoke late in the day, the stable was empty and the Mother and Child nowhere to be seen.

Was it all a strange and beautiful dream? Yet when she looked at the cloak wherein she had wrapped the King of the World, it was bright with stars.

She longed to find the Mother and Child once more, and passing out onto the hillside, she looked for a sign to show the way they had gone. And lo! Before her in the moonlight she saw the footsteps of a woman shining in the dew. With love and wonder Bride followed those steps, for she knew that the King of the Elements was her guide.

Day dawned and the footsteps were no longer to be seen. But she heard the cry of a seabird and before her lay a gleaming pool fringed with rowan trees. She stood once more on the hills of Iona and the murmuring of the sea was in her ears. The Foster-Mother of the Prince of Peace had returned to the waiting Druids with the words for which they longed, "Behold! The King of the Elements has come to birth!"

Another ancient tradition recounts that each morning when Bride ascended Dun I to wash herself in the waters of the well, as she did so, the sun would immediately stretch out a beam of golden light upon which she could hang her cloak. To this day, there continues to exist a widespread belief that if one drinks of the waters of this well on Iona seven times, one will remain eternally youthful.

* * *

In addition to the various places which they discovered in the world of nature as being suitable for spiritual enlightenment, human beings out of their instinctive insight have also from most ancient times created man-made settings for ritual activities. These included such artifacts as menhirs, dolmens, obelisks, stone circles, burial mounds and chambers, temples, tombs, high crosses, round towers, and other similar structures, devoted to sacred purposes. From the simple plowing of a field (agriculture by definition is a sacred act performed on earth in service of the divine) to the construction of a mighty temple or pyramid, in every instance the path has the possibility of leading to an experience of the spiritual, regardless of the wide diversity in the form of the structures involved.

From remotest time, numberless unhewn monoliths of stone, commonly known as menhirs, were set up and erected for widely differing purposes. When these single monoliths were grouped together, they formed dolmens or cromlechs, consisting of an enormous stone slab spanning over several vertical standing stones, often marking a burial site. One way of understanding the significance of these mysterious vertical monoliths as they stand isolated in the landscape, is to observe in them an appeal to one's memory, to recall one's spiritual origin, or to bring to mind a noteworthy event out of the past.

For those to whom the seasonal rhythms of the earth were of prime importance, it was essential to observe the movements and changing relationship of the sun, moon, and other planets. To this end, the stone circles of the Celtic world were erected by ancient peoples, possibly out of the wisdom acquired from the sun mystery centers of Atlantis. On the basis of this knowledge, their priests were often able to predict with extraordinary accuracy planetary eclipses and various events connected with the world of the stars. Among the many well-known stone circles in Britain are Stonehenge near Salisbury, Castlerigg at Keswick in the Lake district, the ring of Brodgar in the Orkneys, and the stone circle at Callanish on the island of Lewis.

Numberless burial chambers and mounds can be found throughout the Celtic lands, created as repositories for the bodies of the deceased, and bearing impressive witness to the Celtic conviction of immortality. The shape of these tombs varies with the location, from the beehive type in the south to the stone ship-burials in the north. The ability to shape, cut, and engrave spiral patterns in the massive slabs used in the construction of these tombs indicates a unique, often sophisticated mastery in the use of tools and materials in times long anterior to the Celtic era.

In Ireland the round barrows and chambered cairns date from earliest pre-Christian times. Certainly the most famous domed tumulus to be found is that at Newgrange in the Boyne River valley near Drogheda, only twelve miles distant from Tara. Newgrange comprises a huge man-made mound of stones and earth almost three hundred feet in diameter and some seventy feet high. The outstanding feature of Newgrange is the orientation of its central burial place, reached by a gently winding passage about seventy feet in length, enclosed by great upright blocks of stone, covered with carvings. This passage is arranged in such a manner that at dawn on the winter solstice, December 21, the first rays of the rising sun penetrate into the darkness, reaching fully into the back niche of the central chamber. The most impressive carved spiral stone in all Ireland stands at the entrance to this largest of neolithic burial mounds.

A much earlier form of the well-known Irish round towers of Christian times is that of the broch, impressive remains of which still exist in the Orkney and Shetland islands. The many round towers found in Ireland, built largely between the eighth and thirteenth centuries, and generally located in proximity to a church, were used as places of refuge, as watchtowers, as storehouses, and later as bell towers, corresponding to the *campanille* of the churches of Italy. (See the classic work on this subject by Henry O'Brien, *Atlantis in Ireland*, originally published London 1834, reprinted by Steinerbooks, NY, 1976; and also Jakob Streit's *Sun and Cross*, Floris Books, Edinburgh, 1984.) A Scottish example of such a round tower, adjoining the cathedral at Brechin, is almost a hundred feet high and was built approximately A.D. 1000.

At Monasteboice in County Louth, Ireland, an outstanding grouping of chapels, round towers, and high crosses is preserved. These crosses are unique in their remarkable state of preservation and splendid array of carved details, depicting biblical scenes as well as elaborate Celtic ornamentation. An equally impressive group exists at Glendalough, a site of Druid fame, today a remarkably well-maintained national park in County Wicklow.

In early times on Iona, nearly two hundred high crosses stood on the soil of this sacred island. By the time of the Protestant Reformation the majority of these had been thrown into the waters of the Sound of Mull. Nevertheless, three of Iona's crosses, each of them unique in itself, have been preserved: the crosses of St. Martin and St. John standing in front of the Iona Abbey, and McClean's cross, carved from a single thin slab of slate, near the parish church, notable for its delicacy of detail.

These Celtic crosses are generally referred to as *sun* or *resurrection* crosses. This expresses their distinctive feature in that the sun circle, as the central motif, surrounds and unites the arms of the cross. At the same time, the rays of the sun are free to shine through the openings between circle and cross, at such moments transfusing the solid stone with golden light, the glowing circle thus becoming the crown of Christ's victory.

Another significant feature is often placed at the top of these crosses, in the form of a small, chapel-like structure, or as in the Ahenny burial ground, where rounded beehives are carved in the stone. Here the bee becomes an ever-present image of unremitting industry, commitment to community, and complete selflessness, characteristic of the ideals of the monks themselves, in harmony with the sun motif given by St. Benedict: *labore et orare*, to labor is to pray.

In conclusion it becomes clear that, across the long ages stretching from the most ancient mysteries to our time, the Celtic high cross continues to reveal itself as a true Easter or Resurrection cross, proclaiming the ever-continuing activity of the forces of the new mystery teaching: "Christ is rising." In this miraculous metamorphosis, the symbol of death is thus transformed into that of the Tree of Life, of that Life which extends throughout the aeons.

❦ 3 ❧

Esoteric Secrets of Fingal's Cave

Fingal's Cave, a structure which had been architecturally formed entirely out of the spiritual world, stood before them, mirroring their own musical inner depths . . . . Those who beheld it were reminded of mysterious ancient destinies, when they saw how Nature herself appeared to have constructed something which may be likened to a wonderful cathedral. It is formed with great regularity, its countless pillars towering aloft; the ceiling arching above being constructed of the same stone, while below the bases of the pillars are washed by the inrushing foaming waves of the sea, which ceaselessly surge and undulate with thunderous music within this mighty temple. Water drips steadily from stone formations above, striking the truncated stumps of the stones below, making melodious magical music. Such phenomena exist there.

—*Rudolf Steiner, March 3, 1911*

 Among all sites devoted to initiation practices directed toward spiritual enlightenment, caves, some of them natural, others shaped by humans, have been most widespread and frequently used from the earliest ages of prehistory. Caves have long been centers around which many legends and superstitions have gathered, and throughout history have evoked the awe and wonder of humanity. They have been used in all periods of human life on earth as dwellings, as places of refuge and protection, as burial sites and for religious inspiration.

References to caves in mythology, folk traditions, and fairy tales abound among widely separated peoples the world over. For example, in Babylon, the royal magicians were initiated in underground caves, as was also the usual practice throughout most of the ancient world. In Persia, caves formed the setting for rituals of the Mithras cult. In classical Greek times, cave temples were dedicated to Zeus, Pan, Dionysus, and Pluto, and were also famous as places where oracular teaching was given, for example in Corinth and Delphi. In Roman mythology, caves were described as the abode of sibyls and nymphs. It is well known that the famous seven sleepers of Ephesus passed their long repose in a cave, while a number of mountains are even today believed to be inhabited by sleeping hosts of fairies, dragons, the little people, as well as by heroes and rulers such as Roland and King Arthur, "the King who will return."

In the biblical world, it is reported that when Lot went up out of Zoar, he dwelt in a cave with his two daughters. The five kings of the Canaanites took refuge from Joshua, as did David from Saul, in the caves of Israel. In Genesis we read that Abraham purchased the field of Ephron and the cave therein, to be the burial place for his wife Sarah, for Abraham himself, and later for Isaac and Rebekah, Jacob and Leah. One of the most dramatic conversations in the entire Old Testament took place in the cave on Mt. Horeb, when Elijah spoke with God and heard "the still small voice." The visit of the Magi, bringing gifts to the Jesus child of the Matthew Gospel, is often depicted in art as occurring before a cave, in which the birth itself took place.

Caves appear in the literature of many periods of world history and in a number of countries. A well-known example from Greek mythology concerns Odysseus and his adventure with the one-eyed cyclops Polyphemus who dwelt in a cave in the southwest corner of Sicily. Another Greek myth recounts that one of the twelve labors of Heracles took place in a cave. The ancient myths of Iran describe the ten-year cave initiation of Zoroaster, who experienced on the one hand, the nightmarish terrors of dark Ahriman and the blessing of enlightenment through Ahura-Mazdao on the other.

Talmudic tradition recounts that when Moses was being prepared for his spiritual leadership, this was done under the guidance of the initiate Jethro, who sent him for this purpose to the cave of Serval on the slopes of Mt. Sinai. This awesome cave had been a sacred place of initiation from time immemorial (see Edouard Schuré, *The Great Initiates*, Rudolf Steiner Publications, N.Y., 1961, p. 202 ff.).

In the wealth of graphic illustrations created by artists to represent the transmuting processes of alchemy, particularly between the fifteenth and eighteenth centuries, a high point of development was attained in the texts of Robert Fludd and Jacob Boehme, both illustrated by the Dutch engraver Johannes Theodosius deBry and others. These elaborate drawings, particularly those by deBry, depict magical Rosicrucian and Kabbalistic processes, portraying the indispensable elements of the occult activity taking place in physical substances within the confines of cavelike retorts, flasks, bottles, kettles, and furnaces. These alchemical instruments required most careful manipulation in order for successful results to be obtained and acted as enclosures for hermetical initiation processes taking place within them. (See Allen, P. M., *A Christian Rosenkreutz Anthology*, Rudolf Steiner Publications, New York, 1968.)

In Goethe's *Fairy Tale of the Green Snake and the Beautiful Lily*, the snake recalls her earlier experiences in the underground cavern, which, although she did not know it then, was to be a place of spiritual initiation:

> In the chasm, where she often crawled hither and thither, she had made a strange discovery. For although in creeping up and down this abyss, she had never had a ray of light, she could well enough discriminate the objects in it by her sense of touch. Generally she met with nothing but irregular productions of nature; at one time she would wind between the teeth of large crystals, at another she would feel the barbs and hair of native silver, and now and then carry out with her to the light some straggling jewels. But to her no small wonder, in a rock which was closed on every side, she had come on certain objects which betrayed the shaping hand of man. Smooth walls on which she could not climb, sharp regular corners, well formed pillars, and what seemed strangest of all, human figures which she had entwined more than once and which appeared to her to be of brass, or of the finest polished marble. All these experi-

ences she now wished to combine by the sense of sight, thereby to confirm what as yet she only guessed. She believed she could illuminate the whole of that subterranean vault by her own light, and hoped to get aquainted with these curious things at once. She hastened back; and soon found, by the usual way, the cleft by which she used to penetrate the Sanctuary.

(The complete text of *The Fairy Tale* by Goethe is to be found on page 121, Allen and Allen, *The Time Is at Hand*, Anthroposophic Press, 1995.)

In more recent times, the cave motif has appeared in a number of guises in books written for children and adults alike. Among these are Mark Twain's *The Adventures of Tom Sawyer* where McDougal's Cave is a hiding place for a treasure of robbers' gold. In Johann Wyss's *Swiss Family Robinson*, the island cave provides the family with shelter, safety, and adventure, while in his novels about the Red Indians, James Fenimore Cooper makes use of caves in the unfolding events of his *Leather Stocking Tales*. More than this, modern scholars have observed that the language spoken by Cooper's characters bears a striking resemblance to that spoken in *The Poems of Ossian*, as presented by James Macpherson.

In *The Poems of Ossian*, there are a number of instances where caves are depicted as an important part of the unfolding narrative. Among these are three examples from the Epic of Fingal:

>—Cuthullin from the cave of Cromla, heard the noise of the troubled war.

>—Allad! said the chief of Cromla, peace to thy dreams in the cave.

>—Then Gaul and Ossian sat with Swaran, on the soft green banks of Lubar. I touched the harp to please the King, but gloomy was his brow. He rolled his red eyes toward Lena. The hero mourned his host. I raised mine eyes to Cromla's brow. I saw Cuthullin, the son of generous Semo. Sad and slow, he retired from his hill, towards the lonely cave of Tura. He saw Fingal victorious, and mixed his joy with grief. The sun is bright on his armor. Con-

nal slowly strode behind. They sunk behind the hill, like two pillars of the fire of night, when winds pursue them over the mountain, and the flaming heath resounds! Beside a stream of roaring foam his cave is in a rock. One tree bends above it. The rushing winds echo against its sides.

Our physical world abounds in caves, most of them of great antiquity. Since prehistoric times many of these have been occupied by human beings, who have left behind them unique traces of their mythology, as well as of their daily lives and activities. In recent times the wonders of the Franco-Cantabrian caves, located in western France and Spain, those of Lascaux being the best known, have stirred the interest of artists and archeologists alike. In this part of the world there are about five hundred caves, approximately one-third of which contain paintings, engravings, and sculptures. Though no artistic works have been thus far discovered in the remainder of these caves, numerous artifacts have been found, pointing to the fact that these caverns were doubtless used for ordinary living rather than for sacred purposes alone.

Painted images represented on the walls of Lascaux and other caves depict the fauna of their period—deer, bison, wild cattle, horses, mammoth, wild boars, and bears, as well as varying activities of human beings. In some instances the figures are drawn in full color, while others are engraved in line or shown as sculptures in relief or in the round.

Of similar interest are the caves of the Bushmen in southern Africa whose traditional legends surrounding the figure of their God-being Mantis, are vividly portrayed in the writings of the late Sir Laurens van der Post.

In 1991, Marlo Morgan's book *Mutant Message Down Under* appeared, published by HarperCollins N.Y. In this highly evocative account describing an American physician's walk with the nomadic aboriginals of the Australian outback, the climax of her four-month journey occurs when the group allows her to experience their most sacred place below the surface of the earth, which as they explain to her "has kept our people alive since the beginning of time." This awe-inspiring visit to a vast complex of underground caverns brings her into intimate contact with evidences of primeval wisdom as expressed in artifacts of extraordinary antiquity, beauty, and unbelievable perfection. Touching upon what at times may be almost fictional, this book nevertheless can hardly fail to impress the reader with the author's awareness of the seriousness of the times in which we live and the urgent problems confronting humanity today.

Participants in the Idriart Festival held in Slovenia, summer 1997, had the opportunity to visit the famous cave of Postojna, lying some eighty kilometers (fifty miles) southwest of Lubljana. This cave was made famous by Dante, who in the late thirteenth century found inspiration here for themes in his *Divine Comedy*. Upon entering a small aperture set into a verdant mountain slope, the visitor travels some one hundred fifty meters deep into the earth, partially on hands and knees, before arriving in the central space of the cave itself, a lofty structure approximately thirty meters long, and in part fifteen meters high.

In the December 1996 issue of *Perspectives, The Christian Community Journal* (Aberdeen), Rachel Shepherd's article "Journey to India" presents a fascinating aspect concerning the role caves play and have played in the spiritual experiences of humanity. Her contemporary account is based upon a journey together with a team of medical workers in spring 1996, to visit the Patal Bhuvaneswar caves, located near the Nepalese border, and considered to be one of the major sources of the Ganges River.

For many centuries the Indian people have descended into these vast caves, a number of them as yet not determined, going there to perform holy rituals of ancient initiation. Bearing flaming torches to light their way, and with the guidance of ropes, chains, and one another, they descended far into the depths of the earth, their path at times leading them through the tiniest apertures. Eventually their way opened out into a series of extraordinary caves in whose natural rock formations, what seemed to be the whole mythology and history of ancient India stood before them, livingly portrayed in stone. From earliest times the forces of nature had been represented for them in the form of the thousand-footed elephant, the cobra, the tongue of the dog, the entrance to the other world with its choice of four doors,

Ganesha the elephant-headed god and the hair of Shiva, down which trickles the water which eventually becomes the Ganges River.

It is said that this cave is the home of the spiritual forces that created the world, and is the early dwelling place of Shiva, the god of destruction and regeneration alike, the ultimate creator. The lingams of the world, remarkable ellipsoid forms containing powerful creative and healing forces, are believed to have their earthly origins here. Clearly this was a setting for ancient initiation and is today one of the world's unique places of wisdom, healing, and spiritual enlightenment. People who have been fortunate enough to have spent a longer time in these caves have recounted that during their visits the gods had stepped forth from the rock walls and become living beings.

In North America many caves in widely separated parts of the country are treasured for their unique and dramatic beauty, as well as their extraordinary size and extent. Among these, one of the most famous is Mammoth Cave in Kentucky, the combined length of all its accessible avenues being about 150 miles, its many cataracts dropping from heights of up to 160 feet, amid walls wonderfully draped with stalactitic tapestry. Its spectacular stalagmites and stalactites abound in vivid colors and forms, today their age-old darkness now illuminated for the benefit of visitors from far countries of the world.

The Navaho, Hopi, and Apache Native Americans of the southwestern United States, have long used caves located in faces of cliffs as places of habitation, as well as venues for highly secret rituals. In the Ohio River region of the United States, the serpent mounds often depict the snake and egg, this motif having doubtless been brought from Mexico, where the serpent divinity Quetzalcoatl has played a leading role for many centuries. These mounds can be regarded as "inverted cave structures."

One of the most fascinating caves in Britain is Wooky Hole, located west of the city of Wells in Somerset. Here, where the river Axe issues from the foot of a steep cliff, the remains of ancient lead mines are to be found, showing traces of prehistoric human habitation. A wealth of traditions regarding elemental beings, specters, and ghosts, have been associated with Wooky Hole for generations.

*   *   *

From these and similar examples, it can be seen that the antiquity, number, and variety of caves and grottos used throughout the millennia by humanity as places of habitation, refuge, and earthly settings for spiritual enlightenment is practically limitless. However in this present volume, it is our intention to concentrate on what is perhaps one of the most famous caves in all the world. It is located on the island of Staffa in the inner Hebrides off the west coast of Scotland. Long known as Fingal's Cave, it is rightly regarded as one of the wonders of the natural world.

The island of Staffa lies almost due north and south, is three-quarters mile long by one-third mile wide, includes an area of seventy one acres, its highest point being one hundred and thirty five feet above sea level. Except for the northeastern shore, the coast is rugged, caves having been carved out by storm, tides, and ocean. The entire island of Staffa is of volcanic origin, the last remnant of a fiery stream of lava. The geological formation of the island is threefold in character. First is a basement of tufa, on which rest colonnades of basalt, in pillars, forming the faces and walls of the principal caves, while the latter in turn are overlaid by a mass of amorphous basalt. Fingal's Cave, best known of all caves on Staffa, is situated on the southern side of the island, facing Iona six miles to the south. It is two hundred and twenty seven feet long, forty two feet wide, sixty six feet high and twenty five feet deep at ebb. On its western side the pillars are thirty six feet high, on the east side eighteen feet high, and from its mouth to its deepest point a pavement of broken pillars runs along the east wall of the cave.

As innumerable visitors have recounted, under ideal atmospheric conditions, its beauty is unique. The play of color is exquisite, the basalt combining every tint of warm red, brown, and rich maroon. Seaweed and lichens paint the cave green and gold, while the lime that has filtered through has etched the pillars here and there a pure snow-white. The floor of the cave is formed by the green sea, out of which the columns rise on either side with a regularity so perfect as to suggest the hand of man, rather than the work of nature. Not far distant is the landing stage, near the Clamshell Cave, where the columns have been eroded to form a rocky pathway running the entire way to Fingal's Cave itself.

The ceaseless murmur of the sea may possibly have caused the cave to be known among the Scottish Gaels as *uamb bhinn* or the "musical cave." Donald B MacCulloch in his *The Wondrous Isle of Staffa* (Oliver and Boyd, Edinburgh, 1957), describes it in this fashion:

> The peculiar musical sounds emitted from Fingal's Cave, apart from the regular boom of the waves striking it, are probably caused by the air being trapped in a hole underwater, from which it can be seen bubbling up on a calm day. This aperture is located a little below the base of the columnar structure at the inner end of the cave, and may form the mouth of a further cavity or cave. These musical sounds are heard more distinctly when one is a short distance from the mouth of the cave, while inside the cave itself the unceasing boom of the waves and the numerous echoes formed thereby, seem to drown the higher notes.

Prof. Sir A. Geikie, the well-known geologist, has stated that there can be little doubt that this etymological explanation of the name of Fingal's Cave is correct. The volume of air driven into the internal cavity by the impact of the water is under the pressure sometimes of several tons to the square inch of surface. When the pressure is suddenly relaxed by the sinking of the waves, the imprisoned air at once rushes out into favorable chinks and passages, giving rise to musical sounds as when a trumpet is blown. This is but one of several characteristics that distinguishes Fingal's Cave as unique among other well-known caves, making it one of the wonders of the natural world.

* * *

It seems remarkable that, as we shall see, it was just during the closing decades of the eighteenth century that a number of highly significant occurrences took place. It appears to have been more than a matter of chance that, when in 1762 *The Poems of Ossian* first appeared, this event was almost immediately followed by others of equal or perhaps greater importance. Joseph Banks rediscovered Fingal's Cave in 1772; Goethe, as part of a lifetime of intense cultural activity, wrote his *Fairy Tale of the Green Snake and the Beautiful Lily* in 1795 and completed

Faust shortly before his death in 1832; and meanwhile in the same years, the long and often bitter controversy between the Neptunists and Vulcanists erupted, the subject of which concerned the role of water and fire in the creation of the earth and its phenomena.

During the later part of the eighteenth and throughout the greater part of the nineteenth century, there arose in Britain and elsewhere what later came to be known as the "Ossianic controversy." This involved an attack on the integrity of James Macpherson as author of *The Poems of Ossian*, by men such as Dr. Samuel Johnson and Malcolm Laing. On the other hand, Macpherson was staunchly defended by Dr. Hugh Blair and a host of Gaelic enthusiasts. This outer confrontation was ostensibly based on whether or not *The Poems of Ossian* were translations of genuine Gaelic productions from the earliest Christian centuries, or whether they were creations by the poet James Macpherson himself, in which case his claims could be properly dubbed fraudulent.

As in so many confrontations, in this one also, the real underlying issue did not involve authenticity or authorship as such, but was an expression of the attitude of certain contemporaries of Macpherson who were blinded by ecclesiastical prejudice, shortsighted in their own literary points of view, or were caught up in conflicting tides of nationalism. Such people were hardly in a position to successfully achieve a solution to this problem, which involved an awareness of profound unseen factors posed by the issue as a whole. However, today with the help of further insights available, it is possible to grasp the entire Ossianic question in a quite new, constructive, and objective light. (See for instance, Gaskill, Howard, ed., *Ossian Revisited*, Edinburgh University Press, 1991.)

During the same period that this controversy was at its height, a not dissimilar and yet far more profound struggle was being waged by thinkers in Britain and on the Continent. It concerned a matter that had challenged philosophers in times long anterior to the eighteenth century, outwardly appearing totally unrelated to *The Poems of Ossian* themselves. The underlying cause or origin of this controversy lay far back in prehistory, and involved one of the most profound subjects known to humanity, in other words the nature of the relationship between water and fire, an apparently totally irreconcilable problem. In the light of spiritual research, this contradiction can in a certain sense bring about a solution and thus bridge the apparently unbridgeable. This possibility the ancients knew full well, but due to the limitations of technical knowledge in their time, were unable to reach what today can be a satisfactory solution of the problem.

Goethe was a pioneer in his portrayal of this problem in the classical Walpurgis Night scene, in his *Faust, Part II*, where in the encounter between the classical figure of Thales (624–546 B.C.) and that of Anaxagoras (500–428 B.C.) he depicts something of a clarification of this problem from a cultural-spiritual standpoint. The entire drama of *Faust*, including this particular scene, was most ably translated into English by the late George Madison Priest (Knopf, N.Y., 1941), long a lecturer on Goethe at Princeton University. We have prefaced the text of this scene by Dr. Priest's explanatory note as follows:

> By the Upper Peneus, Anaxagoras, a Plutonist, according to Goethe, and Thales, a Neptunist, the two sages, differ in their views of the way in which Nature works. Anaxagoras was an Athenian philosopher, a friend of Pericles, and a teacher of Euripedes. Thales, also a philosopher, advocated the theory that the earth floats on primeval waters which gave and give birth to all beings and all life. The following lines from the drama indicate implicitly Goethe's attitude toward a lively dispute which took place during Goethe's later life about the origin of the earth's surface: whether the surface of the earth came about through volcanic action by means of fire or as a deposit of primeval seas, that is, was of Neptunist origin. Goethe stood with both feet on the side of the Neptunists, since their theories coincided closely with his way of thinking and, believing in the quiet rule of nature in its "gentle progress," he was deeply opposed to the violent and revolutionary.

Faust, Part II, Act II, Scene 4

Anaxagoras: You will not let your rigid mind be bent
              Is ought more needed to make you assent?

Thales:	To every wind the wave bows fain enough,
	But from the rugged rock it holds aloof,
Anaxagoras:	Through flaming gas arose this rock we're seeing.
Thales:	In moisture came organic life to being.
Anaxagoras:	Have you, O Thales, even in one night
	Brought such a mountain out of slime to light?
Thales:	Nature with all her living, flowing powers
	Was never bound by day or night or hours.
	By rule she fashions every form and hence
	In great things too there is no violence.
Anaxagoras:	But here there was! Plutonic savage fire,
	Aeolian vapors force, explosive, dire,
	Broke through the ancient crust of level earth
	And a new mountain straight way came to birth.

During the lifetime of Goethe, two outstanding figures emerged in the history and development of geology. Around these men, what was to become a celebrated controversy developed and was carried on with great vigor into the later decades of the eighteenth century. This primarily concerned the origin and nature of basalt, a substance that plays a major role in the structure of Fingal's Cave.

The first of these men, Abraham Gottlob Werner (1750–1817), father of German geology, the great proponent of the Neptunist teaching, based his theory on the idea that the earth is predominantly created and sustained by water. His enthusiasm and eloquent presentations, at a comparatively early age, drew around him students from all parts of the world. For forty years he devoted his active and indefatigable industry to the department of minerology at Freiburg, so that it became one of the great centers of scientific learning in Europe.

While these theories of Werner were finding wide acceptance on the European continent, the subject was being approached from a new and independent point of view by a Scotsman, James Hutton (1726–1797) of Edinburgh. In his major work, *Theory of the Earth with Proofs and Illustrations*, 1795, he advanced the Vulcanist theory of creation, in which he taught that the world was largely formed by fire and volcanic activity. Here we have once again the same figures of Thales (in the role of Werner, the Neptunist) and Anaxagoras (in the role of Hutton, the Vulcanist), as Goethe depicts them in an artistic manner in *Faust,* confronting one another in a controversial situation.

As the first three decades of the nineteenth century drew to a close, due to much scientific investigation on the part of leading geologists in a number of countries, Neptunism (creation by water), rapidly declined in influence, while Vulcanism (creation by heat), came steadily to the fore where it has remained into our own time.

This was by no means the first time that these two critical elements of fire and water confronted each other, for the folklore, legends, and myths of peoples the world over recount in various guises the stories of the destruction of Lemuria by fiery volcanic action, and of Atlantis by catastrophic floods. In the world of the ancient orient, one finds the profoundly significant Yin and Yang figures. Moreover during the later middle ages, through the Renaissance and on into the age of the Reformation, water and fire played a vital role in the Alchemical Rosicrucian initiation processes.

Fingal's Cave, including the basalt of which it is formed, is a most remarkable manifestation of the blending of these two creative powers. The Vulcanist or fire principal was more active in the initial creation of Staffa, followed as it was by an ever increasing intensification of the Neptunist or water principal, which has continued to exert its influence on the basaltic formations to the present time.

Basalt is one of the oldest geological names in current use and includes a large variety of types of igneous rock belonging to the basic subdivision. Dark in color, often weathering to brown and rich in magnesium and iron, an unusual characteristic of this group of rocks is the perfection with which many of them are columnar in form, often called basaltic jointing. The distribution of basalts is worldwide and in some places they occur in immense masses and cover great areas. In Hawaii and Iceland they are the prevalent lavas, and the well-known jointed columnar basalts of Skye, Staffa, and Antrim (the Giants' Causeway) form a southward extension of the Icelandic volcanic formation.

A striking feature of the basaltic columns on Staffa is their tendency to present themselves in orderly hexagonal shaftlike forms. Their unvarying, unique characteristic is their six-sidedness. The geometric form of the hexagon can be likened to its "community building" quality, since they can be placed side by side without limit. An example of this is the form and structure of the honeycomb of beehives. Engineers have found that this hexagonal form set up in this way is the most perfect shape for the creation of a vacuum. As a result of this vacuum-forming principal, in our time honey has been taken from the ancient tombs in Egypt, where it has remained unspoiled and uncontaminated for thousands of years.

The figure of the hexagon is built up of six equilateral triangles. The polygon, which can be formed within the hexagon by connecting the six corners, is called a hexagram, and consists of two interlocking equilateral triangles. This is known everywhere as the Old Testament Star of David, the Star of the Annunciation. All angles in this polygon are multiples of six and the resulting hexagram expresses perfect balance, purity, and harmony between the ascending and descending triangles, thus representing the above and below—that is, spirit and matter intermingled in visible form. This sequence can be represented thus:

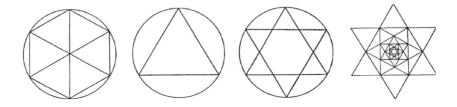

In ancient Hebrew occult tradition, the number six signifies beauty, proportion, balance, and harmony manifested in the laws of equilibrium. In the traditional teaching of the Kabbala by Abraham Abulafia (thirteenth century), in the ancient Throne Mysticism, as well as in the Zoharic doctrine of Issac Luria (sixteenth century), the figure six as found in the hexagon, stands in the place of Tiphereth—beauty— and is manifested in the region of the heart in the meditative picture of cosmic man, Adam Kadmon.

Numbers were considered central to the Pythagorean view of creation. One was regarded as the basic unit from which all others were created. It was therefore symbolic of the divinity, of reason, and of all that was eternal and unchanging. Even numbers were feminine and symbolized things essentially belonging to the earth. Odd numbers were masculine and symbolized things belonging to the heavens.

If we do not consider the number 1, the first perfect number is 6—that is, its proper divisors are 1, 2, and 3 and 1 + 2 + 3 = 6. The next perfect number is 28. As the first perfect number, 6 was of special significance for both Jewish and Christian writers in ancient times. We read of the six days of creation, the six lambs without blemish, Goliath's height as six cubits, the six boards of the tabernacle, the six steps of King Solomon's throne, the six measures of barley, and so on. Along with seven, the number six also passed into the mystical deliberations of Christian writers. St. Augustine suggested that six as a perfect number has an important existence independent of the rest of creation. He wrote: "God created all things in six days because this number is perfect and it would have been perfect even if the work of the six days did not exist."

In the Apocalypse of St. John, the sixth church signifies the sixth epoch of civilization called Philadelphia, the epoch of brotherly love, which according to many indications will be the age of a true harmonious spiritual life of wisdom and love among humankind.

All of the foregoing touches upon only a small portion of the vast esoteric wisdom lying behind the hexagonal forms, outwardly manifested in the structure of Fingal's Cave. This knowledge is the golden key, which can unlock for us the secrets of the physical forms of Fingal's Cave, shaped as Rudolf Steiner has said, "entirely out of the spiritual world itself."

This profound insight of Steiner echoes lines written by William Wordsworth in 1833, while as poet laureate he visited Staffa on a tour of the Hebrides. As a result of his visit, he later wrote four poems entitled the "Cave of Staffa." The first of these poems in a certain sense anticipates what Steiner was to say in his address in 1911 concerning the origin of the forms of Fingal's Cave. The text of Wordsworth's poem follows:

Cave of Staffa

We saw, but surely, in the motley crowd
Not one of us has felt the far-famed sight;
How could we feel it? Each the other's blight,
Hurried and hurrying, volatile and loud.
O for those motions only that invite
The Ghost of Fingal to his tuneful Cave
By the breeze entered, and wave after wave
Softly embosoming the timid light!
And by one Votary who at will might stand
Gazing and take into his mind and heart,
With undistracted reverence, the effect
Of those proportions where the Almighty hand
That made the worlds, the sovereign Architect,
Has deigned to work as if with human Art!

26. Pre-Christian dolmen, County Down, Ireland.

27. Carved stone at Newgrange. (By permission of Little, Brown and Company)

28. Carved stone at Newgrange. (By permission of Little, Brown and Company)

29 and 30. Newgrange—exterior and interior views. (By permission of Little, Brown and Company)

31. Stonehenge, England, a drawing from Higgens's Celtic Druids, 1827.

32. LEFT: Monasteboice. County Louth, Ireland. Muireadach's Cross, early tenth century.

33. BELOW: Rosicrucian alchemical furnace—Geber, seventeenth-century drawing.

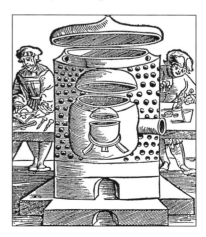

34. Ahenny Cross with beehive motif, Ireland—east face.

35. Ahenny Cross with beehive motif, Ireland—west face.

36. *The Mountain of the Philosophers*, Rosicrucian drawing, 1604.

37. Twelfth step in the alchemical process, drawing, 1624.

38. Saturn unifying fire and water, seventeenth-century Rosicrucian drawing.

39. Assia Turgeniev, underground-cavern scene from Goethe's *Fairy Tale of the Green Snake and the Beautiful Lily*, written 1795.

40 and 41. Lascaux cave paintings, bison and horse, southern France.

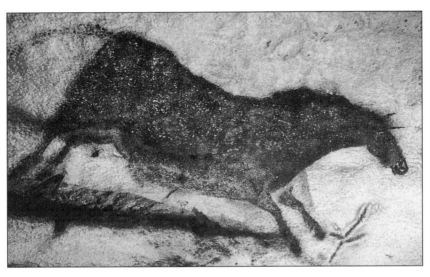

42 (ABOVE) and 43 (BELOW). These ancient rock formations, at Boynton Canyon in Sedona, Arizona, long a center of mystery worship by Native Americans, startlingly prefigure architectural forms of Greek temples and of the Goethenaum, Switzerland. *(Photographs by Pete Gollogly)*

44. Clach Ossian, reputed burial stone of Ossian beside River Almond in the Sma' Glen, Perthshire.

GLEN ALMAIN; or, The Narrow Glen
(William Wordsworth, composed probably 1803; published 1807)

In this still place, remote from men,
Sleeps Ossian, in the NARROW GLEN;
In this still place, where murmurs on
But one meek streamlet, only one:
He sang of battles, and the breath
Of stormy war, and violent death;
And should, methinks, when all was past,
Have rightfully been laid at last
Where rocks were rudely heaped, and rent
As by a spirit turbulent;
Where sights were rough, and sounds were wild,
And everything unreconciled;
In some complaining, dim retreat,
For fear and melancholy meet;
But this is calm; there cannot be
A more entire tranquillity.

Does then the Bard sleep here indeed?
Or is it but a groundless creed?
What matters it? — I blame them not
Whose Fancy in this lonely Spot
Was moved; and in such way expressed
Their notion of its perfect rest.
A convent, even a hermit's cell,
Would break the silence of this Dell:
It is not quiet, is not ease;
But something deeper far than these:
The separation that is here
Is of the grave; and of austere
Yet happy feelings of the dead:
And, therefore, was it rightly said
That Ossian, last of all his race!
Lies buried in this lonely place.

[Note: Wordsworth visited the Sma' Glen (see illustration 44) in 1803.]

45. Abraham Gottlob Werner
(1750-1817), Neptunist, father of
German geology.

46. James Hutton (1726-1797),
Vulcanist, father of creation by
heat theory.

47. Mythological
union of fire and
water, ancient
Indian drawing.

❦ 4 ❧

Who Is Fingal?

Those who upon discovering Fingal's Cave, and who had a feeling for the mysterious things which once took place here, were reminded of that hero, who once upon a time, as one of the most famous individualities of the West, guided destiny here in such a unique manner, and whose fame was sung by Ossian his son, who like Homer, was a blind bard.

However . . . this created a quite different conception of humanity than we have today. This earlier conception was based upon the view that the human being was united with spiritual powers sounding forth from the whole world of Nature. He could not look upon a storm or see a flash of lightning, he could not hear the thunder or the surging of the sea, without sensing that out of all the activities of Nature, spirits worked who were connected with the souls of the past, with the souls of his own ancestors. Thus the activity of Nature was at that time something altogether different than for us today. . . .

Out of such wisdom the finest sons from the different clans— that is, those who had the strongest connection with the spirits of the past, who more than others allowed these spirits of the past to live in their deeds—were chosen as a select band. And those who had the strongest clairvoyant forces were placed at its head. This group had to defend the core of the Celtic people against the peoples of the surrounding world. One of these leaders was the clairvoyant hero who has come down to us under the name of Fingal. How Fingal was active in the defense of the ancient spiritual beings against those who wished to endanger them—all of this was handed down in ancient songs, heard out of the spiritual world, the songs of the bard Ossian, Fingal's son, so that it remained alive even into the sixteenth and seventeenth centuries. What Fingal achieved, what his son Ossian heard after Fingal had ascended into the spiritual realms, what their descendants experienced in Ossian's rhythms and sounds, with all this they ever and again ensouled their deeds. This it was which worked on so mightily even into the eighteenth century. And we shall gain a conception of this when we perceive how Ossian lets the voice of his father, Fingal, sound forth in his songs.

—*Rudolf Steiner, March 3, 1911*

 Over the years it has been noted that the question most frequently asked by the many visitors to Staffa has been and remains: "Who was Fingal, for whom the cave is named?" However, before approaching this question, it is important to recognize that the ancient literature of the Gaelic branch (Scottish and Irish) of the Celtic people falls into three cycles or groups. First is the mythological cycle which deals with the history and folklore of Scotland and Ireland. The second or Cuchullin cycle, contemporaneous with the earthly life of Christ, is generally referred to as the time of the golden age of Irish romance. It is in this cycle that stories of the reign of King Conchobar are included.

Rudolf Steiner indicated that the spiritual sight of the Druids of this time was such that they were able to observe events taking place at a given moment in far distant parts of the world. An example of this is the Gaelic story of Conchobar and his Druid, which took place at the very moment of Christ's crucifixion. In 1924, William Butler Yeats (1865–1939) included the following version of this tale in his *Later Poems*, drawing on the manuscript of the twelfth-century *Book of Leinster* now in Trinity College, Dublin:

There was a King in Ireland called Conchobar, who had once been struck by a ball made out of the dried brains of an enemy and hurled out of a sling, and this ball had been left in his head, and his head had been mended with a thread of gold because his hair was golden. Keeling, a well-known writer of the time of Elizabeth I gives the rest of the legend in this form. . . . " In that state he did remain for seven years, until the Friday on which Christ was crucified, according to some historians. When he saw the unusual changes of the creation, and the eclipse of the sun, and the moon at its full, he asked Bucrach, the Leinster druid, who was along with him, what it was that brought that unusual change upon the planets of heaven and earth. "Jesus Christ, the Son of God, who is now being crucified," said the Druid. "That is a pity," said Conchobar, "for if I were in his presence, I would kill those who were putting him to death." And with that he drew his sword, and rushed at an oak grove which was convenient to him, and began to cut and strike at the oaks. And from the very excesses of his fury which seized him, the ball started out of his head, and some of the brain came after it, and in that way he died.

The third cycle of Gaelic literature concerns us most directly when we consider the question: "Who was Fingal?" Known as the Ossianic cycle, the time of its origin has been placed some three hundred years later than that of the Cuchullin cycle. It is from these two cycles that James Macpherson drew much of his material, which forms the basis for a number of his *Poems of Ossian*, published in London 1762.

In the Cuchullin cycle, the "I," the ego of the individual comes to the fore. The struggles involve champion against champion, whereas the hosts of the armies as such count for little. In contrast, in the Ossianic cycle, we meet a group or band of heroes whom Rudolf Steiner characterizes as "those who were chosen to defend the core of the Celtic people against the peoples of the surrounding world." These were known as the Feine, Fianna, or the Fingalians. They formed what might be called a kind of standing army, with Fingal at their head, whose task was to defend the land and its people from invasion. However, it should be noted that Fingal by no means outshone the others in valor and strength, but that it was he alone who possessed a profound degree of spiritual wisdom. From what has already been written

above, it thus becomes clear that in Fingal we have not only a historical figure out of Irish and Caledonian mythology, but a spiritual leader
of more than human dimension, the enlightened clairvoyant hero of
the Celtic people.

Fingal is represented in history as a great warrior and champion of
the good, but in the popular folklore tradition he belongs to the race
of the giants and has supernatural powers. The great Scottish histo-
rian, Hector Boece (1465–1536), writing in about the year 1500, describes Fingal as a giant some seven cubits in height (about eleven
feet), presents him as a Scotsman, fixes his date around A.D. 450, and
tells us further that he is renowned for stories similar to those told
about King Arthur. William Dunbar (1460–1522) a poet contemporary with Boece, describes him in a line from one of his poems: "Ay
whan he dansit the warld wald schog" (ay when he danced the world
shook).

The well-known scholar, Standish O'Grady in his *History of Ireland*,
1884, places the Fingalians back in the dawn of Irish history as: "gigantic figures in the dusky air. . . . With one foot on lofty Mt. Cromlech
and the other on black Mt. Crommeal, Fingal could take up the water
in his hands from the River Lubar."

Rudolf Steiner in his address of March 3, 1911, opens his reading of
selections from *The Poems of Ossian* in this translation by James
Macpherson:

> The king stood by the stone of Lubar. Thrice he reared his terrible
> voice. The deer started from the fountains of Cromla. The rocks
> shook on all their hills. Like the noise of a hundred mountain-
> streams, that burst, and roar, and foam! Like the clouds, that gather
> to a tempest on the blue face of the sky! so met the sons of the
> desert round the terrible voice of Fingal. Pleasant was the voice of
> the king of Morven to the warriors of his land. Often had he led
> them to battle; often returned with the spoils of the foe!

In John F Campbell's (1822–1885) *Popular Tales of the West Highlands* (4 volumes, 1862,) is described how the people imagined the race
of giants to have originated:

An old king of Erin, hard pressed by his enemies, consulted his druid as to the best course to pursue. He advised him to marry 100 of his tallest men to the same number of tallest women, then again to intermarry 100 of each sex of the tallest of their descendants and so on, to the third generation. This would give him a gigantic race enabling him to cope with any foe. This was done and by the third generation a gigantic race was the result. Their leader and ruler was named Cumal, who became the father of Fingal.

William Butler Yeats in his introduction to Lady Augusta Gregory's *Gods and Fighting Men*, one of the foundation stones of Celtic revival literature, creates a beautiful imagination of the Fingalians:

We think of Fingal and his companions as great-bodied men with large movements, that seem, as it were, to be flowing out of deep influences. They are men that have broad brows, and quiet eyes full of confidence in a good luck, that proves everyday afresh that they are a portion of the strength of things. They are hardly so much individual men, as portions of universal nature itself, like the clouds that shape and reshape themselves momentarily, or like a bird between two boughs, or like the gods that have given the apples and the nuts; yet this but brings them nearer to us, for we can remake them in our image as we will, and the woods are the more beautiful for the thought.

According to the old Irish mythologies, the birth of Fingal, also referred to as Fionn or Finn, came about in this manner. At the time he was born, his father, Cumal, son of Trenmor, had been killed in battle by the sons of Morna, often mentioned in Macpherson's eighteenth-century reconstruction of *The Poems of Ossian*. His mother the beautiful long-haired Muirne, daughter of Tadhg, chief Druid of Conn, did not dare to keep her son, because as rightful heir to the throne he would have been killed. Therefore she gave the newborn child into the care of two women, Bodhmall, a female Druid, and Liath Luachra, his nurse. They reared him in a secret place in the forest, caring for him and training him in running, leaping, swimming, hunting, fishing, and the bearing of arms. When he was seventeen, they said to him one day: "It is best that you leave us now, for the sons of Morna wish to kill you." Obediently Fingal wandered off by himself, and after many trials, reached his father's brother Crimall, having been able to rescue his father's magical treasure bag on the way.

After saying farewell to Crimall, Fingal went on to learn versification from Finegas, a fisherman-poet then living on the banks of the River Boyne. Although Finegas had diligently fished for seven years, he had never succeeded in catching the mythological salmon of all knowledge, because it was believed from an old prophecy that this particular salmon would be caught only when the hero Fingal himself would appear. The ancient tale continues:

> When Finegas the fisherman cast his line in Fingal's name, he at once caught a gigantic salmon, but it was too large for Finegas. Impatiently, Fingal took the line and landed a yet larger salmon. Then the fisherman recognized Fingal and said that he must roast the salmon with the fish on one side of the stream, and the fire on the other, nor must he use any wood in the process. Fingal set fire to some sawdust, and the wind blew a wave of fire over to the fish and burnt a spot on it. Fingal put his thumb on the black spot, it burnt him and at once he put his thumb into his mouth. In that instance he knew everything: past, present, and future alike were revealed to him.

After many further adventures, it was at Teamhair or the Hill of Tara that Fingal eventually recovered his rightful patrimony and kingship. Some of the outstanding followers who shared in the unfolding exploits of the Fingalians were:

Fingal—King of Morven
Ullin—the bard of Fingal
Gaul (Goll)—leader of the clan Morna
Ossian—son of Fingal, the renowned warrior and blind bard
Fergus and Ryno—sons of Fingal, warriors and poets

Oscar—son of Ossian, the bravest of the Fingalians, youthful and
  kindhearted
Diarmid—the handsomest, the Adonis of the Fingalian mythology,
  whose slaughter by a wild boar is one of the best known myths of
  the Ossianic cycle
Caoilte—Fingal's nephew, the swiftest of the Fingalians (like the
  Greek Hermes—Mercury)
Connal—petty chief of Togorma
Conan Maol—the fool of the Fingalians

In the words of Ossian himself, the following passage from *Fingal, an Epic Poem, Book IV*, identifies some of the leading Fingalians mentioned above:

> Fingal, like a beam from heaven, shone in the midst of his people.
> His heroes gather round him, he sends forth the voice of his power.
> "Raise my standards on high, spread them on Lena's wind like the
> flames of a hundred hills! Let them sound on the winds of Erin and
> remind us of the fight. Ye sons of the roaring streams, that pour from
> a thousand hills, be near the king of Morven! Attend to the words of
> his power! Gaul, strongest arm of death! O Oscar of the future fights!
> Connal, son of the blue steel of Sora! Diarmid of the dark brown
> hair! and Ossian, king of many songs, be near your father's arm!" We
> reared the sun-beam of battle, the standard of the king. Each hero's
> soul exulted with joy, as waving it flew on the wind. It was studded
> with gold above, as the blue wide shell of the nightly sky. Each hero
> had his standard too, and each his gloomy men.

Probably no modern writer has portrayed the figure of Fingal with
equal spiritual acumen and profound insight as has Lady Augusta Gregory (1852–1932). As a founder of the world famous Abbey Theater in
Dublin, she was one of the most beloved of those connected with the
Celtic revival movement early in our century. Remembered today as
Patroness of the Arts in Ireland, she wrote many popular stories and
plays based upon themes and traditions from Irish mythology and folklore. Outstanding among her works is *Gods and Fighting Men*, 1904,

from which the following accounts regarding Fingal and the Fingalians have been chosen:

> As to Fingal himself, he was a king and a seer and a poet, a druid and a knowledgeable man, and everything he said was sweet sounding to his people. And a better fighting man than Fingal never struck his hand into a king's hand, and whatever anyone ever said of him, he was three times better. And of his justice it used to be said, that if his enemy and his own son had come before him to be judged, it is a fair judgment he would have given between them. And as to his generosity it used to be said, he never denied any man as long as he had a mouth to eat with, and legs to bring away what he gave him. And he left no woman without her bride-price, and no man without his pay, and he never promised at night what he would not fulfill on the morrow, and he never promised in the day what he would not fulfill at night, and he never forsook his right-hand friend. And if he was quiet in peace, he was angry in battle, and Ossian his son, and Oscar his son's son, followed him in that.

In this description are shown the ideal characteristics of a true initiate leader, harmonizing with Rudolf Steiner's description of "the clairvoyant hero, who has come down to us under the name of Fingal." Moreover around Fingal were gathered a gifted group of people. These not only included the fighting heroes named above—the Fingalians—but also many others as well:

> And the number of the Fingalians of Ireland at that time was seven score and ten chief men, every one of them having 3 x 9 fighting men under him. And every man was bound by three things, to take no cattle by oppression, not to refuse any man as to cattle or riches, and no one of them to fall back before nine fighting men. And there was no man taken into the Fingalians until he knew the twelve books of poetry. . . . Besides the fighting men, Fingal also had with him his five Druids, the best that ever came into the west, Cainnelsciath, of the Shining Shield was one of them, that used to bring down knowledge from the clouds in the sky before Fingal,

and that could foretell battles. And Fingal had his five wonderful physicians and his five high poets and his twelve musicians, that had among them Daighre, son of Morna, and Suanach, son of Senshenn, that was Fingal's teller of old stories, the sweetest that ever took a harp in his hand. And he had his three cup-bearers, and his six door keepers, and his horn-players, and the stewards of his house and his huntsman, Comrag of the five hundred hounds and his serving-men that were under Garbhcronan of the Rough Buzzing. . . . And there were also fifty of the best sewing women brought together in a rath, under the charge of a daughter of the King of Britain, and they used to be making clothing for the Fingalians through the whole of the year. And three of them, who were King's daughters, used to be making music for the rest on a little silver harp. And there was a very great candlestick of stone in the middle of the rath, for they were not willing to kindle a fire more than three times in the year, for fear that the smoke and the ash might harm the needlework.

And of all his musicians, the one Fingal thought most of was Deireoil, the Little Nut, that came to him from the Sidhe (the fairy folk). It was at Slieve-Nam-Ban for hunting, was the time he came to him. Sitting down he was on the turf-built grave that is there, and when Fingal looked around him he saw a small little man about four feet in height standing on the grass. Light yellow hair he had, hanging down to his waist, and he was playing music on his harp. And the music he was making had no fault in it at all, and it is much that the whole of the Fingalians did not fall asleep with the sweetness of its sound. He came up then, and put his hand in Fingal's hand. "Where do you come from little one, yourself and your sweet music?" said Fingal. "I am come," he said, "out of the place of the Sidhe in Slieve-Nam-Ban, where ale is drunk and made, and it is to be in your company for a while I am come here." "You will get good rewards from me, and riches and red gold," said Fingal, "and my full friendship, for I like you well." "That is the best luck ever came to you Fingal," said all the rest of the Fingalians, for they were well pleased to have him in their company. And they gave him the name of the Little Nut, and he was good in speaking, and he had so good a memory he never forgot anything he heard, east or west. And there was no one but must listen to his music, and all the Fingalians liked him well. And the five musicians of the Fingalians were brought to him, to learn the music of the Sidhe he had brought from that other place, for there was never any music heard on earth, but his was better. These were the three best things that Fingal ever got, the Little Nut from the house of the Sidhe in Slieve-Nam-Ban, and the two hounds, Bran and Sceolan that were without fault.

(Now follows Lady Gregory's version of the birth of Bran and Sceolan:) Fingal's mother Muirne came one time to Almhuin, and she brought with her Tuiren, her sister. And Iollan, a chief man of the Fingalians of Ulster, was there at the time. He gave his love to Tuiren, and asked for her hand in marriage, and brought her to his own house. . . . But before Iollan made that marriage, he had a sweetheart of the Sidhe, Uchtdealb of the Fair Breast, and there came great jealousy on her when she knew he had taken a wife. And she took the appearance of Fingal's woman messenger, and she came to the house where Tuiren was and she said, "Fingal sends health and long life to you, and bids you make a great feast. Come with me now, so I can speak a few words with you, for there is hurry on me."

So Tuiren went out with her, and when they were away from the house the woman of the Sidhe took out her dark druid rod from under her cloak, and gave her a blow of it, that changed her into a hound, the most beautiful that was ever seen. And then she went on bringing the hound with her to the house of Fergus. And it is the way Fergus was, he was the most unfriendly man to dogs in the whole world, and he would not let one stop in the same house with him. But it is what Uchtdealb said to him: "Fingal wishes you life and health, Fergus, and he says to you to take good care of his hound till he comes himself. Mind her well for she is with young, and do not let her go hunting when her time is near, or Fingal will be no way thankful to you." "I wonder at that message," said Fergus, "for Fingal knows well there is not in the world a man has less liking for dogs than myself. But for all that, I will not refuse Fingal the first time he sent a hound to me."

And when he brought the hound out to try her, she was the best he ever knew, and she never saw a wild creature she would not run down, and Fergus took a great liking for hounds from that time out. And when her time came near, she gave birth to two whelps.

And as to Fingal, when he heard his mother's sister was not living with Iollan, he called to him to go looking for Turien. Iollan went to the hill where Uchtdealb was, his sweetheart of the Sidhe, and told her the way things were with him. "If you will give me your pledge to keep me as your sweetheart to the end of your life, I will free Tuiren." So Iollan gave her his promise, and she went to the house of Fergus, and she brought Tuiren away, and put her own shape on her again, and gave her to Fingal. And as for the two whelps, they stopped always with Fingal, and the names he gave them were Bran and Sceolan.

The Fingalians' Farewell:

As with the famous farewell words of King Arthur to those gathered around him "the old order changeth, and yieldeth place to the new," so the comparable poignant scene included in the Fingal epic, as related by Lady Gregory, leaves one with a strong impression that, although the Finaglians may fade away, they will one day return as "the bearers of the new."

It was the last time Fingal and Ossian and the rest of the Fingalians were gathered together for hunting, for battle, for chess-playing, for drinking or for music, for they all wore away after that, one after another. . . . And with that Ossian kissed Fingal his father and bade him farewell, and to the rest of the Fingalians, and he went up then on the horse with Niamh. And the horse set out gladly, and when he came to the strand he shook himself and neighed three times, and then he made for the sea. And when Fingal and the Fingalians saw Ossian facing the wide sea, they gave three great sorrowful shouts. And as to Fingal, he said, "it is my grief to see you going from me, and I am without a hope, ever to see you coming back to me again." . . . And as to Fingal, there are some say he died by the hand of a fisherman, but it is likely that is not true, for that would be no death for so great a man as Fingal, son of Cumal. And there are some say he never died, but is alive in some place yet.

And one time a smith made his way into a cave he saw, that had a door to it, and he made a key that opened it. And when he went in he saw a very wide place, and very big men lying on the floor. And one that was bigger than the rest was lying in the middle, and the Dord Fiann, his magic hunting horn beside him. And he knew it was Fingal and the Fingalians were in it. And the smith took hold of the Dord Fiann, and he could hardly lift it to his mouth, and he blew a very strong blast on it. And the sound it made was so great, it is much the rocks did not come down on him. And at the sound the big men lying on the ground shook from head to foot. He gave another blast then, and they all turned on their elbows. And a great dread came on him when he saw that, and he threw down the Dord Fiann, and ran from the cave and locked the door after him, and threw the key into the lake. And he heard them crying after him, "you left us worse than when you found us." And the cave was not found again since that time. But some say the day will come when the Dord Fiann will be sounded three times, and that at the sound of it, the Fingalians will rise up as strong and as well as ever they were. And some say Fingal, son of Cumhal, has been on the earth now and again, since the old times, in the shape of one of the heroes of Ireland. And as to the great things he and his men did when they were together, it is well they have been kept in mind through the poets of Ireland and of Alban, the ancient kingdom of Celtic Scots.

Against the background of these and other well-known folk traditions surrounding the name of Fingal, it is clear why the great cave on the isle of Staffa is known today as Fingal's Cave. As the "musical cave" it continues to speak its word of creative power and majesty, just as today the name Fingal still remains the embodiment of the rich heritage portrayed in the figure of one of the most famous spiritual initiates of the Western world.

Seven years after the death of James Macpherson, translator of *The Poems of Ossian*, the following poetic imagination and tribute by P. B.

Homer was published as part of his *Observations on a Short Tour in Scotland 1803*:

> Fingal in his spacious hall
> That echoes with the ocean's thundrous fall,
> Whose waves on Staffa's massy pillars roar,
> And shake with deafening noise the caverned shore,
> There Morven's mighty chief we hear,
> His valiant arm reclining on his spear,
> While thousand demigods that gather round,
> Hear their noble leader's animated sound;
> Or tune their harps to love and soft desire,
> Striking with joy the golden lyre.
> In song they pass the night and chant the praise,
> Of high-born warriors famed in ancient days.

From James Macpherson,
Fragments of Ancient Poetry, 1760, no. 8

By the side of a rock on the hill, beneath the aged trees, old Ossian sat on the moss; the last of the race of Fingal. Sightless are his aged eyes: his beard is waving in the wind. Dull through the leafless trees he heard the voice of the north. Sorrow revived in his soul: he began and lamented the dead.

How hast thou fallen like an oak, with all thy branches round thee! Where is Fingal the King? Where is Oscar my son? Where are all my race? Alas! In the earth they lie. I feel their tombs with my hands. I hear the river below murmuring hoarsely over the stones. What does thou, O river, to me? Thou bringest back the memory of the past.

The race of Fingal stood on thy banks, like a wood in fertile soil. Keen were their spears of steel. Hardy was he who dared to encounter their rage. Fillian the great was there. Thou Oscar wert there, my son! Fingal himself was there, strong in the grey locks of years. Full rose his sinewy limbs; and wide his shoulders spread. The unhappy met with this arm, when the pride of his wrath arose.

The son of Morny came; Gaul, the tallest of men. He stood on the hill like an oak; his voice was like the streams of the hill. Why reigneth alone he cries, the son of the mighty Corval? Fingal is not strong to save; he is no support for the people. I am strong as a storm in the ocean; as a whirlwind on the hill. Yield son of Corval; Fingal, yield to me. He came like a rock from the hill, resounding in his arms.

Oscar stood forth to meet him; my son would meet the foe. But Fingal came in his strength and smiled at the vaunter's boast. They threw their arms round each other; they struggled on the plain. The earth is ploughed with their heels. Their bones crack as the boat on the ocean, when it leaps from wave to wave. Long did they toil; with night, they fell on the sounding plain; as two oaks, with their branches mingled, fall crashing from the hill. The tall son of Morny is bound; the aged overcame.

Fair with her locks of gold, her smooth neck, and her breasts of snow; fair, as the spirits of the hill when at silent noon they glide along the heath; fair, as the rain-bow of heaven; came Minvane the maid. Fingal! she softly saith, loose me my brother Gaul. Loose me the hope of my race, the terror of all but Fingal. Can I, replies the King, can I deny the lovely daughter of the hill? Take thy brother, O Minvane, thou fairer than the snow of the north!

Such, Fingal! were thy words; but thy words I hear no more. Sightless I sit by thy tomb. I hear the wind in the wood; but no more I hear my friends. The cry of the hunter is over. The voice of war is ceased.

5

Druids and Bards

While the migrations from Atlantis toward the east were taking place, those Druid priests who had remained behind in the west, were able to exert a harmonizing influence upon the people living there in small family groups. What they thus gave, lived on in the bards who followed them. However, we shall only understand what worked through these bards, when we realize that here the most elementary passions were united with the ancient power of "second sight" into the spiritual world, and that those heroes who at times fought passionately against other clans, perceived impulses coming from the spiritual world which directed them.

Such an active connection between the physical and the soul realms cannot be conceived of today. When a hero raised his sword he believed that a spirit out of the air guided it, and in this spirit he beheld an ancestor who in earlier times had fought upon this same battlefield, and who had gone up yonder in order to help from there. In their ranks both sides felt their ancestors aiding them. However they not only felt them, but also heard them spiritually. It was a wonderful conception which lived in these people: that the heroes had to fight and shed their blood on the battlefield, that after death they ascended into the spiritual world, and that their spirits then vibrated as tone, sounding through the air as spiritual reality.

Those who had proven themselves in battle, but at the same time had trained themselves so that they could listen to what sounded to them out of the spirit as the voice of the past, who were blind to the physical plane, the physical world, no longer able to see the flashing swords, they were nevertheless highly honored. One of these heroes was Ossian. When the warriors wielded their swords, they were aware that their deeds would resound further in the spiritual world, and that bards would later appear who would preserve all this in their songs. This was a living perception to these people.

—*Rudolf Steiner, March 3, 1911*

 The mysterious depths of the great Caledonian forests, deeply shrouded in darkness, formed the setting for the cultivation of the spiritual wisdom of the ancient Gaelic Druids. Their teachings exerted a harmonizing, balancing influence upon those members of the blood-related groups who came under their tutelage.

In book five of his *De Bello Gallico* Julius Caesar (100–44 B.C.) included important information about the Druids and their teachings. He indicated that for the most part the Druids included men of rank and dignity, thus forming the learned and priestly class of society. They were also the leading interpreters and guardians of the law. On those who refused to submit to their decisions, they could inflict severe penalties, even involving exclusion from society itself. Two major privileges that they enjoyed were exemption from military service and freedom from taxation.

The period of training required of a druidic pupil is said to have been around thirty years and all instruction was given orally. Among the subjects included in their training were the physical sciences as understood at that time, geography, astronomy, and the theology of nature, according to which they taught that the human soul is immortal.

Certain parts of this instruction were given in places of lonely seclusion—, for example, in stone beehive type cells, on storm-swept uninhabited islands, as well as in remote caves and dark underground labyrinths. These dark enclosures can be pictured as images of the physical human body, where soul and spirit often lie imprisoned, and can be released only through most rigorous disciplined training. Later this led to a misunderstanding of the exile of certain monastic candidates to lonely inhospitable places by their superiors, whereas in reality, this was a positive part of their training and inner development. Such exile was referred to in the words of St. Columba of Iona when he speaks of "a dark cell without light."

Although regular gatherings of Druids were held at various times in what today is Scotland, England, Wales, and Ireland, once every year according to Caesar and others, a solemn general assembly for purposes of final initiation into "the great mysteries of druidism" was held in Gaul at Carnotum (Chartres) in the region of the Carnutes.

The Gauls frequently made human sacrifices to their gods. Their laws required that at least one senior Druid be present at such events in order to ensure that the sacrifice would be acceptable. Marcus Tullius Cicero (106–43 B.C.) also wrote about the Druids, indicating their occult skill as teachers, soothsayers, and prophets, and describing how at certain critical moments they threw themselves between two opposing armies, thus sacrificing their lives in order to bring about peace.

The Roman writer Pliny the Elder (A.D. 23–79) reported that the Druid's activities included the practice of medicine and sorcery. Traditionally oak groves were regarded by them as being particularly sacred, since whatever grew on such trees was thought to be a gift from heaven. Especially the mistletoe was held by them as an object of veneration, because it grows not on soil but in the air, and lives on the life of the tree to which it is attached. The mistletoe blossoms not in spring but in the autumn, at the time when other plants decay. Used in a certain way its extracts could heal many illnesses and it was discovered that it could have an effect on one's consciousness, lifting one above the usual bodily senses, thus at those times enhancing the power of spiritual sight. According to Virgil, the Golden Bough, which the Greek Sybil instructed Aeneas to discover, was probably the mistletoe. This plant enabled him to enter Hades, the world of the dead, by changing his conciousness so that he could meet there with the shades of his ancestors. Thus in solemn holy rituals the Druid priests, dressed in white robes, cut the mistletoe from the oak branches with sacred golden sickles.

In addition to what was described in classical Roman accounts, the Druids played a significant part in the Gaelic life and literature of Ireland and Scotland well into the early Christian centuries, when their role was gradually taken over by bards, poets, and certain early Christian saints. In chapter 4 the story is told of Conchobar and his Druid Cathbad (also known as Bucrach), at the moment of the crucifixion of Christ. It is reported that at the court of Conchobar no one had the right to speak before the Druids had spoken, a custom doubtless practiced in other royal courts at that time.

Although in early Gaelic writing, the Druids are often represented as opposing the spread of Christianity, this was not always the case. For example, in one of his later writings, St. Columba of Iona speaks thus of "Christ my Druid" in these lines:

> I adore not the voice of birds,
> Nor sneezing, nor things of this world.
> For my Druid is Christ, the Son of God,
> Christ, Son of Mary, the Great Abbot,
> The Father, the Son, and the Holy Spirit.

This is a clear indication of the regard with which the Druid's wisdom, knowledge, and learning remained alive even into the latter part of the sixth century and beyond. In a lecture given on December 9, 1923, Rudolf Steiner observed that:

> The druid mysteries of Hibernia belong to those we refer to as the great mysteries, because the initiation of the students gave them a survey, an outlook over life before birth and after death. At the same time, it gave them a survey of cosmic life into which man is enwoven and out of which, in the course of time, he is born. Thus man learned to know the microcosm, i.e. to know himself as a being of body, soul and spirit in his relation with the macrocosm. He also learned to know the coming into being, the weaving, the arising, the passing away and the constant metamorphosing of the macrocosm. These Hibernian mysteries reached their full flower in the period which preceded the Mystery of Golgotha, but in these mysteries the Christ was spoken of as the one who was to come, just as later men spoke of the Christ as of one who had gone through events in the past. . . .

There was in fact upon this island [Ireland], which was later to go through so many trials, a center of the great mysteries, a center of Christian mysteries before Golgotha, in which the spiritual sight of a man living before the Mystery of Golgotha was directed toward it. After the Mystery of Golgotha had taken place, when in Israel the wonderful events of the experiences of Christ Jesus on Golgotha had come to pass, great festivals were held within the communities of the Hibernian mysteries. And what had occurred in actual fact in Israel, was portrayed in a multitude of spiritual pictures on the island of Hibernia, although these pictures themselves were but a memory of the past. However, the people experienced the Mystery of Golgotha spiritually in pictures at the same time on the island of Hibernia, as the Mystery of Golgotha came to pass historically in Israel. In Hibernia was spiritually seen what took place before the physical eyes of men in Israel, at the beginning of our era.

The Druids were actually not Christian in our modern sense of the word. Even the greatest of them were essentially pre-Christian witnesses of the Sun-Being's descending path leading toward earthly incarnation. Spiritual destiny required that they wait until the great burst of illumination that had flashed upon their inner vision from Palestine to Ireland, could at last focus itself in the teachings of a Patrick or a Columba.

In contrast to the Druids, the Gaelic bards, particularly in the highlands of Scotland and Ireland, were concerned above all with the creative power of the word in speech and song. This involved rhythm, sound, and poetry in relation to the preservation and transmission of folklore, deeds of the heroes, and stories of their people. The bards were traditionally divided into three main groups: the first celebrated victories and sang hymns of praise; the second chanted the laws of the people; and the third recited family histories and genealogies in verse form.

Though little physical evidence of the ancient Druid Hibernian mystery wisdom remains today, it was principally the bards who preserved in song and poetry some of the wisdom of the past in the form of allegory and image. Knowledge of spiritual wisdom was cultivated by the Druids and experienced by them in their rituals held in sacred groves, and in the sunlight and shadow of their stone circles, open to the starry heavens, as at Stonehenge and similar places.

In contrast, through their preoccupation with music and poetry and the warmth of their intuitive heart experiences, the bards often sought the darkness and mystery of caves and underground sanctuaries, which at times is said to have expressed itself in physical blindness as with Homer, Ossian and others. Therefore many bards are said to have been blind because "they had looked on beauty and had not feared truth." Indeed one may say that their blindness was in reality the fruit of seeing truth itself. Echoes of this sound in the following passage from *The Poems of Ossian*, Son of Fingal:

> And a voice calls to us on the wind. We have passed away like flames that have shone for a season. And another cries: beside the stone of Mora I shall fall asleep. The wind whistling in my gray hair shall not awaken me. Depart on thy wings, O wind! Thou canst not disturb the sleep of the bard. The night is long and his eyes are heavy. Depart thou rustling blast. Shalt thou then remain, thou ancient bard, when the mighty have failed? But my fame shall remain and grow like the oak of Morven, which lifts its broad head to the storm and rejoices in the course of the wind!

The above lines express the essence of the inner life of the Celts and the Gaels, of the bards in particular. To them the ideal was the only reality, and physical objects were but the vesture or shadow of the invisible world surrounding them. Camille Flammarion (1842–1925), the famous French scientist and astronomer, wrote that "observation proves that the soul world is as real as the material. The Gael and the Celts in general, appear to be endowed in larger measure than any other people with the psychic faculty."

These words of Flammarion point to the well-known faculty of second sight or *an taibhsearachd* in the Gaelic—long associated with the highlanders of Scotland. In his *Description of the Western Isles* published in 1705 the writer Martin Martin (ca. 1660–1719) of Skye gives many details of second sight, which include the following:

The sight is a singular faculty of seeing an otherwise invisible object without any previous means used by the person who sees it for that end. They neither see nor think of anything else except the vision as long as it continues. At the sight of the vision the eyelids of the person are opened and the eyes continue staring until the object vanishes. The faculty of second sight does not lineally descend in a family, although some families do seem to have it handed down through several generations. The faculty is not communicable, however it can be passed from a seer to one who has not the gift, by placing his foot on the other's foot, or by some other physical contact.

A spark of fire appearing on the breast or arm, was the forerunner of a dead child to be seen in the arms of those persons. An empty seat where a man was sitting meant his early death. Seers were of both sexes. The seer would sometimes fall into a swoon. . . . Children, horses, and cows could see the second sight as well as men and women advanced in years. The seers are very temperate. Both sexes are free from hysterical fits, convulsions, and other distempers of that sort. No mad men are to be found among them, nor any instance of self-murder. A man drunk never sees the second sight, nor is he a visionary in other affairs of life. They are not impostors, and although illiterate, they are altogether devoid of design. They have nothing to gain by it. The people are not credulous, but believe because of the fulfillment of the prediction. Some seers are persons of birth and of education. Some visions are fulfilled in the lifetime of the seer, other visions not till after his death. It is not enviable to be a seer, as it is not considered to be a very reputable gift. A preventative was to wear a plant called "fuga demonum" sewn in the neck of the coat.

Another writer, William MacLeod, of Hamar, Skye, under his penname of Theophilus Insulanus, published A *Treatise on the Second Sight, Dreams and Apparitions*, in 1763, the year following the appearance of *The Poems of Ossian*. In this book MacLeod writes:

The Roman poet Lucretius (96–55 B.C.), through the tenets of his philosophy, was obliged to maintain that the soul did not exist separate from the body, nevertheless makes no doubt of the reality of apparitions, and states that men have often appeared after their death. This I think very remarkable. He was so impressed with this fact which he could not deny, that he was forced to account for it by a most remarkable notion. He tells us that the surfaces of all human bodies are perpetually flying off from their respective bodies, one after another, and that these surfaces, or thin cases that included each other, whilst they are joined together in the body, like the skins of an onion, are sometimes seen entire, when they are separated from it, by which means we often behold the shapes or shadows of persons who are either dead or absent.

In this connection one is reminded of numerous descriptions given by Rudolf Steiner, in his fundamental books and lecture cycles, concerning the nature of the physical, etheric, and astral bodies of the human being.

In a paper read before the Gaelic Society of Inverness in 1919, the Reverend Dugald MacEchern, at that time bard to the society, concluded with these words: "To the Hebrew seer cradled on the Nile, it was given in Horeb to behold the burning bush. To the Scottish Gael cradled beside the Atlantic wave and nursed on the breasts of the mountains, it was given to apprehend that ever-living spirit world that penetrates the world of matter."

In the opening book of the epic poem *Temora*, forming a major part of *The Poems of Ossian*, a poetic example of the working of second sight appears. This occurs through the perceptions of old Althan, chief bard of Arth, king of Ireland, who foresees the death of Cormac, the king's son:

> The setting sun was yellow on Dora. Gray evening began to descend. Temora's woods shook with the blast of the inconstant wind. A cloud gathered in the west. A red star looked from behind its edge. I stood in the wood alone. I saw a ghost on the darkening air. His stride extended from hill to hill. His shield was dim on his side. It was the son of Arth. I knew the warrior's face. But he passed away in his blast, and all around was dark. My soul was sad.

At this point returning to his picture consciousness Althan continues:

> I went to the hall of shells. A thousand lights arose. The hundred
> bards had strung the harp. Cormac stood in the midst, like the
> morning star when it rejoices on the eastern hill, and its young
> beams are bathed in showers. Bright and silent is its progress aloft,
> but the cloud that shall hide it, is near. The sword of Arth was in
> the hand of Cormac. He looked with joy on its polished studs,
> thrice he attempted to draw it, and thrice he failed. His yellow
> locks are spread on his shoulders, his cheeks of youth are red. I
> mourned over the beam of youth, for he was soon to set!
>
> "Althan," he said with a smile, "didst thou behold my father?"
> Heavy is the sword of the king, surely his arm was strong. O that I
> were like him in battle, when the rage of his wrath arose! . . . I
> heard Cormac in silence. My tears began to flow. I hid them with
> my aged locks.

In fulfillment of his prophetic second sight, Althan describes the
death of Cormac:

> The sword entered the side of the king. He fell in the halls of his
> fathers. His fair hair is in the dust. His blood is smoking round.
> Mournful are the mountains of Erin, for the chief of the people is
> low! Blest be thy soul, O Cormac. Thou art darkened in thy
> youth!

To the modern reader *The Poems of Ossian* may at first appear turgid
and obscure, the figures depicted may seem to lack reality. However, a
more intimate acquaintance with the representation of such person-
ages as Fingal and his son Ossian the bard, based upon the word pictures of the poems themselves, can give ample evidence of their
unique individuality and qualities as living human beings.

Fingal emerges in an atmosphere of awe, the bearer of heroic
courage and superhuman strength. On the one hand he is filled with
the charismatic power to inspire heroic deeds from his followers in
battle, and at the same time is capable of wise counsel and loyal

friendship. His words often bring comfort and solace to those in need, especially to the women who are so tenderly portrayed in the poems. It is this almost semidivine quality that makes Fingal appear at times as otherworldly, reminding one of Gilgamesh, the ancient Babylonian hero, as being "⅔ divine and ⅓ human." Even his very footsteps shake the earth, his eyes flash with anger, and his gestures brook no denial.

We are like Ferad-artho the warrior, who requested a description of Fingal from his messengers. "Is the King as tall as the rock of my cave? Is his spear a fir of Cluna? Is he a rough-winged blast on the mountain which takes the green oak by the head and tears it from its hill? Glitters Lubar within his strides, when he sends his stately steps along?" However the answer is different from what we may have expected: "He is not as tall as that rock, nor glitters the stream within his strides, but his soul is as a mighty flood, like the strength of Ullin's seas."

The epic poem of *Fingal* is largely concerned with Fingal's heroic repulse and final defeat of Swaran, the would-be Scandinavian invader of Erin. Similarly in the second epic poem, *Temora*, the already aged Fingal, together with the Fingalians, is able to successfully lead an invasion into Erin, there to reestablish the hereditary privileges of the Caledonians, and in doing this removes Cairbar, the usurper, from the throne of Ireland.

How great is the difference between this patriarchal father-figure of Fingal and that of his gentle poet son. The bard Ossian is always present as the faithful narrator and preserver of the account of the heroic deeds and achievements of the Fingalians. Ossian touches the reader deeply through his quality of melancholy reflection, and his atmosphere of "joy in grief" which dominates and pervades his poetry, appearance, manner, and life. Seated peacefully, outside his lonely cave, perhaps similar to that on Staffa, he tunes his harp, assisted in his blindness by his helper Malvina, and plaintively sings his songs of grief, lamenting the loss of his companions of earlier days. His bardic skill appeals above all to the heart, rather than to the head of the reader. In a word, Fingal can be described as the man of action and heroic deeds, while Ossian is the man of feeling and of noble sentiment.

These qualities in *The Poems of Ossian* become even clearer and more accessible when the poems are read aloud. This is due to the fact that they involve rhythm and sound in a unique manner, which becomes clearer when the lines are spoken orally. Such a measured reading enhances the mystical mood implicit in the essence of the poems themselves, a mood that cannot be logically described, but nevertheless is real, palpable, and lasting. This can surround both reader and hearer with an atmosphere transcending mere meaning, bearing its charm to the heart of the individual with inherent strength, power, and beauty.

Something of this must have inspired the eminent Scottish divine Dr. Hugh Blair (1718–1800) to write his *Critical Dissertation on "The Poems of Ossian, Son of Fingal"* in 1763. Hugh Blair had received the degree of Doctor of Divinity in 1757 from the University of St. Andrew. The following year he was promoted to the pastorate of the High Church in Edinburgh, the most important religious position in the Church of Scotland at that time. In 1762 he became the first occupant of the chair of rhetoric and belles lettres at the University of Edinburgh. Later his five volumes of sermons met with great success and were translated into almost every European language. In his *Dissertation*, Dr. Blair characterizes *The Poems of Ossian* thus:

> The two great characteristics of Ossian's poetry are tenderness and sublimity. It breathes nothing of the gay and cheerful kind; an air of solemnity and seriousness is diffused over the whole. His poetry, more than any other writer, deserves to be styled *the poetry of the heart*. It is a heart penetrated with noble sentiments, and with sublime and tender passions; a heart that glows and kindles the fancy; a heart that is full and pours itself forth. . . . The moral of Fingal's behavior is clear and unequivocal; that wisdom and bravery always triumph over brutal force; or another nobler still; that the most complete victory over an enemy, is obtained by that moderation and generosity which converts him into a friend.

This "joy in grief" is one of Ossian's most remarkable expressions, several times repeated. This same formulation is twice used by Homer, in the *Iliad* and the *Odyssey*. However, Ossian makes a distinction between this gratification and the destructive effect of overpowering grief: "There is a joy in grief, when peace dwells in the breasts of the sad. But sorrow wastes the mournful, O daughter of Toscar, and their days are few."

For Dr. Blair, the one regrettable omission in *The Poems of Ossian* is what he describes as Macpherson's failure to mention the existence of a supreme Being. However, in fact, the existence of the totality of nature, is as Goethe indicated repeatedly, ample proof of the working of the spiritual world, behind which stands divinity itself. Therefore in reality Dr. Blair was surrounded by unlimited evidence of the activity of the supreme Being, manifested in the manifold poetic descriptions of nature included in *The Poems of Ossian* themselves.

As already has been indicated, one of the most unforgettable and far-reaching observations given by Dr. Blair in his *Dissertation*, is his statement that "Ossian's poetry, more perhaps than that of any other writer, deserves to be styled *the poetry of the heart*." At the same time, this expression envisions the existence of a Community of the Head and Heart, which can be experienced as a second step following upon that of the Community of the Blood (as described in chapter 2, above.) This second step is a reflection of the life of the soul, living in the immediate present, imaged in the beating heart and the pulsing breath, and is expressed above all in tone and sound, which Rudolf Steiner has characterized as "sound ether." This leads to a living experience of Ossian, the blind bard, seated at the entrance to his cave, his harp held against his breast, his voice tenderly recalling treasures of memory preserved in the rhythm and sound of his poetry:

> Such were the words of the bards in the days of song, when the king heard the music of harps, and the tales of other times! The chiefs gathered from all their hills and heard the lovely sound. They

praised the voice of Ossian, the first among a thousand bards. But age is now on my tongue and my soul has failed. I hear at times, the ghosts of bards, and learn their pleasant song. But memory fails in my mind. I hear the call of years!

—*from the* Songs of Selma

6

Columban Christianity, the Reilig Oran, "Erin's Finest Sons"

It is therefore no wonder that this life, this consciousness of a connection with the spiritual world which sank deep into these people, into the souls of the ancient Celts, is the best preparation whereby they were able to spread the personal divine element throughout the West in their own way and from their own soil. For what they had experienced as violent emotions, what they had heard resounding in the melodies of the spiritual world, prepared them for a later time when they were to bring into the world, sons who revealed these emotions in their souls in a purified and milder form. Thus we may say—it appears as if at that later time Erin's finest sons again heard the voices of their ancient bards singing of what they once had heard out of the spiritual world as the deeds of their forefathers, but it was as if in Erin's finest sons the ancient battle-cries had now been reshaped and clarified, and had become words which could express the greatest Impulse of humankind. . . . We shall imagine these events rightly if we realize that Fingal's Cave acted as a focus-point, mirroring what lived in the souls of these human beings who, through their destiny, were sent hither as if to a temple built by the spiritual beings themselves. Here those human beings were prepared who later were to receive the Christ Impulse with their full humanity, and were here to undergo something highly unique by way of preparation.

—Rudolf Steiner, March 3, 1911

According to the account by Douglas Fraser, published on the front page of the *Scotsman*, Monday, June 9, 1997, the celebration of the fourteen-hundredth anniversary of the death of St. Columba in 597 was observed by an international, ecumenical gathering assembled on the island of Iona, off the western coast of Scotland. Prominent among those attending was the Irish president, Mary Robinson, whose arrival by helicopter was part of a diplomatic pilgrimage, with a view to "strengthening links between the two Celtic countries—Scotland and Ireland—and to sending a clear message back to Ireland about Columba's teaching and example of peace and reconciliation."

Addressing the large gathering of people overflowing the ancient Abbey Church of Iona, Mary Robinson said:

> For me, there are two strong connections with Saint Columba that are very relevant to modern Ireland and Irish people throughout the world. The first is that Columba still remains an important presence and inspiration for the different Christian denominations. Second, he reminds us of how old the links are between Ireland and Scotland. Columba came as someone who wanted to bring Christianity, but also in a spirit of penitence. I also come in that same spirit—a spirit of recognizing that we need to be open and respect the different traditions in Northern Ireland, that we need to build a lasting peace there.

Mary Robinson's remarks were followed by an address given by the Rev. Norman Shanks, leader of the Iona Community. He began by warning his listeners against what he termed the present-day trend of misrepresenting the true nature of original Celtic Christianity. He pointed out that Iona has found itself increasingly attractive to New Agers and the growing numbers who have overimmersed themselves in Celtic mysticism. He stated that the true Columban tradition is about engagement and not about escape, about holding social and spiritual concerns inextricably together, in contrast to the current concept of Celtic Christianity, which tends to sanitize and to romanticize the harsh realities of the conditions in which Columba and his monks lived, demanding and severe as they were in the extreme.

Against the usual background of more than 140,000 visitors to Iona annually—pilgrims, daytrippers, and tourists—the 1997 commemorative gathering also included visitors from Australia, Canada, USA, Africa, Iceland, and many other lands. A number of these visitors were seeking to recapture in their outer journey, an inner journey directed toward God. These twentieth-century "pilgrims" came from Glasgow, Renfrew, Canterbury, Derry, as well as a small group who had journeyed from Rome. With them they brought the tradition of fourteen centuries of pilgrimage to this tiny island, which today has a permanent population of about one hundred persons. They brought banners and pilgrims' crooks, decorated with Celtic symbols, a sunlit positive bond of faith, and talk of ecumenism and reconciliation. They reported that everywhere they had met wonderful hospitality and enthusiasm for their pilgrimage to Iona, the island made famous in the sixth century by St. Columba.

During this year, other commemorative events, most of them ecumenical in nature, were held in numerous places in the British Isles. Outstanding among these was the concert given in Dunkeld cathedral on Saturday, June 7, 1997, entitled "Columba's Music." The program featured the first performance of a work especially composed by William Jackson of Forfar, and sponsored in part by the Scottish Arts Council. The instrumentation included string quartet, various pipes, and ancient Scottish folk instruments, clarsach, as well as Mairi MacInnes, noted Gaelic singer, the Dunkeld parish choir, and a childrens' choral procession. This was augmented by a rich selection of other musical and choral works, readings, and prayers. The evening was opened and closed by the ringing of "The Little Dunkeld Bell," which was cast for Kenneth MacAlpine in the late ninth century, and was rung by the present Rev. Albert Smith.

Dedicated to Columba, patron saint of Dunkeld, in the ninth century the cathedral became the ecclesiastical capital of the new Scottish-Pictish kingdom. It was long the resting place of Saint Columba's relics, transported there by Kenneth MacAlpine in 849, having been removed from Iona in face of repeated Viking raids. The relics remained in Dunkeld until the time of the Reformation. Thus Dunkeld cathedral proved to be eminently appropriate as a setting for this notable commemoration of Columba's death 1,400 years ago.

One may well ask, who was this extraordinary man, whose influence continues to stir human hearts even today, 1,400 years after his death? Since a wealth of biographical works and studies on Columba, his life and influence, are readily available, spanning from the earliest biography written by Adamnan in 692, less than a hundred years after Columba's passing, to the recent book by Ian Bradley, commissioned by the Iona community in 1996, entitled *Columba, Pilgrim and Penitent*, it seems unnecessary to do more here than indicate a few basic details concerning Columba's life and influence.

Born on December 7, 521, at Gartan in County Donegal, Ireland, Columba's father belonged to the then reigning family of Ireland and was also closely allied to the rulers of Dalriada (Argyll, Scotland). His mother Eithne was also of royal blood, related to the kings of Leinster. Tradition recounts that shortly before Columba's birth, she had a vision of the Angel Gabriel, who according to Adamnan "brought to her a mantle of marvelous beauty in which lovely colors of all flowers seemed to have been depicted. After a brief interval the angel asked for it back, took it from her hands, and raising and spreading it out, sent it forth into the empty air." Eithne, saddened by its disappearance, asked, "Why dost thou thus quickly take away from me this lovely mantle?" The angel immediately replied, "For the reason that this mantle belongs to one of such grandeur and honorable station that thou canst keep it by thee no longer!" Adamnan then describes how this mantle increased in size until it seemed to cover all the plains and mountains, and the angel foretold that she should bring forth a son "so illustrious that, like one of the prophets of God, he will be numbered among them, and is predestined by God to be the leader of innumerable souls to the heavenly country."

St. Bridget of Kildare was descended from the same race as that of Columba, but as a child was extremely poor and ever afterward was mindful of those who were suffering and needy, having known poverty herself. Bridget had the gift of prophecy, and foretold the birth of

Columba, saying that: "a young scion would be born in the north, who would become a great tree whose top would spread over Erin and Alba." She died in 523, two years after the birth of Columba.

Columba studied under two of the most distinguished Irish scholars of his day: Finian of Moville and Finian of Clonard. Eventually embracing the monastic life, he entered the priesthood at about thirty years of age. During his time in Ireland, he founded a number of churches and two famous monasteries, Derry and Durrow.

At the age of forty-two, in 563, he left Ireland accompanied by twelve companions, on a mission to Britain, perhaps on the invitation of his kinsman Conall, ruler of Dalriada. Other oft-quoted accounts represent Columba as undertaking this journey following censure expressed against him after the battle of Cooldrevny. Following the admonition of certain members of the Irish clergy, he and his companions were to sail northward in their coracle until at last they would come to a land from which Ireland would no longer be visible. This proved to be the island of Hy, later called Iona, where Columba and his company landed on May 12, 563, the eve of Whitsunday. There they soon established what became a well-known church and monastery, eventually including over three hundred monks and many lay brothers.

About two years later he began his efforts toward the conversion of the northern Picts to Christianity. Crossing to the mainland, he eventually reached Inverness, the seat of Brude, king of the Picts, and there by his preaching, his holy life, and by the performance of miracles, he converted the king and many of his subjects. Finally Columba and his followers brought the whole of northern Scotland to Christianity, and numerous churches and monasteries were built throughout the country.

During these same years, groups of monks left Iona under the leadership of Columban brothers including Kentigern, Gall, Cuthbert, Columbanus, and others, on missionary journeys that took them to the coast of Northumbria, Lindisfarne, and southward across the channel into Brittany, eventually working their way through what is today Switzerland, northern Italy, Austria, and parts of Hungary.

These Celtic monks caused much surprise on the continent, so different were they from the monks people had known before. They were tonsured bare on the front of the head from ear to ear, leaving their long hair behind to flow down on the back. This was known as "the St. John's tonsure" in contrast to "the crown" or "Petrine tonsure." Their eyelids were painted or stained black, and they carried a stout stick or *bachall* and a leathern bag called a *polaires*, hung over the shoulder, in which they kept their precious manuscript copies of the scriptures. They spoke a strange language among themselves, but used Latin to those who understood it and made use of an interpreter when preaching.

Through these many years of expansion and missionary work, the monastery of Iona was always revered as the mother house, the home and spiritual center of what has come to be called Celtic or Columban Christianity, remaining a famous pilgrimage center to this day.

One of the most significant and far-reaching events in the life of Columba as chief ecclesiastical leader was his giving of formal benediction and inauguration to Aidan in 574. Seating Aidan on the druidic black coronation stone at the entrance to the church of Iona, Columba enveloped him in a cloak of saffron yellow, the favorite color of the Columban Christians at that time. He then anointed Aidan's head with oil, proclaiming him successor to Conall as king of Argyll. (There is a tradition that this stone is the same Stone of Destiny on which many kings of Great Britain have been crowned.)

The last years of Columba's life were spent mainly on Iona, where he was already revered as a saint. Today there can be no doubt as to the holiness of his life, as well as the unqualified love and humility that he manifested to God and to his neighbors, as reported in the innumerable accounts of his deeds and miracles.

In the summer of 597, knowing that his end was approaching, on June 8, Columba ascended the little hill above the monastery. Lifting his hands, he gave the island his farewell blessing, in the form of a prophesy: "Iona of my heart, Iona of my love! Where today is the chanting of monks, there will be lowing of cattle. But before the world is ended, Iona will be as it once was." Returning to his cell, he continued his work of transcribing the Psalter. When he finished writing the promise of the tenth verse of Psalm 34: "They who seek the Lord shall want no manner of thing that is good," Columba murmured: "Here I must stop." When the midnight bell sounded for the nocturnal office early on Easter Sunday morning, he blessed the brothers in the church, and sinking before the altar, passed away as if in a gentle sleep. Diormit, his attendant, who was following him from a distance, saw the whole church shining, with angelic light surrounding the saint. As Columba breathed forth his spirit, we are told by Adamnan that "his face remained so ruddy and wonderfully gladdened by the vision of the angels, that it seemed not to be that of one dead, but of one alive and sleeping."

Two particularly important streams began to flow in the life of Christianity in the British Isles, during the period following the departure of the Romans from those lands. One of these streams, as has been described, originated in Ireland, entering Scotland with Columba's arrival on Iona. The other stream had its source in Rome, entering England with St. Augustine's mission to Kent, spreading to Canterbury, where it established its center. It is said that in 596 Pope Gregory, moved to compassion by the faces and fair hair of English slaves in the marketplaces of Rome, asked, "Who are these people?" "They are called Angles" was the reply. At once, the pope said "from now on, let them not be called Angles but *angels*." He therewith sent Augustine to convert Britain to Christianity.

It is a curious and perhaps significant coincidence that the same year when Columba died in Scotland also marked the arrival of St. Augustine in the south of Britain. In matters of ritual, the Columban church agreed with many elements of the Roman church, as practiced by Augustine and his followers. However, there were certain important particulars in which they differed. Among these were: the religious calendar, involving the fixing of the date of Easter; the form of the tonsure; the special relationship that the Columban monks had to the world of nature, reflected in the frequent holding of rituals out-of-doors in natural settings; and the question of the recognizing of the hierarchical structure of the church based in Rome.

One of the principal ways to an understanding of the essence and profundity of Columban Christianity is to see in it an epitome of the three cardinal expressions of the working of the human soul. The first of these workings was the application of the knowledge and learning of the Druids, the result of their nearly thirty years training in what represented natural science of that time. (See page 107, above, in chapter 5.) This can be regarded as the cosmic aspect of Columban Christianity, involving an intense awareness of the role of the Divine as creator and maintainer of all that appears before humanity as sense impressions. This found its expression in intensive study and in their seasonal ritual celebrations. In all of this the biblical Psalms played a pivotal role, their melodies and profundities providing the background out of which the knowledge of the creative working of the spirit could express itself. Psalms 8, 19, 24, 29, and 104 provide clear examples of this. All of the above can be regarded as the *knowledge* aspect of Columban Christianity.

The profound warmth and love of beauty, characteristic of Celtic arts and crafts, found ready application in the lives of Columban monks wherever they went. This manifested itself in their participation in music and choral singing, in poetry, ornamentation and use of color, manuscript illumination, metal work, stone carving, leatherwork, jewelry. Above all, their employment of creative design was the clear expression of the magical metamorphosis, the ever-changing manifestation of the living spirit. The pulsing blood, the enwarmed breath, and the enthusiastic sharing in all that life offered, to the individual as well as to the wider community as a whole, formed the foundation of this second working of Columban Christianity. All of this doubtless originated in the intense artistic life that motivated Columba himself, echoing his great love of the Psalms, in such words as: "O Lord, how I love the beauty of thy house!"

One of the mysteries concerning the monastic rule practiced by the Columban monks in the various centers they established thoughout the highlands, lowlands, and islands of Scotland, concerned the content of their inner meditative life. Undoubtedly, aside from their intense preoccupation with the Scriptures, especially the Gospels and Psalms, the great poetic work written for their use by Columba himself, entitled *Altus Prosator*, formed a central element in their daily life of prayer. This work is remarkable at the same time in that it is an example of a pioneer attempt to give literary form to the Latin language as used in Columba's time, in the same way that Francis of Assisi, more than six hundred years later, was to probe the literary possibilities of the Umbrian dialect in his *Canticle of the Creatures* (see Allen, Paul M. and Joan deRis, *Francis of Assisi's Canticle of the Creatures*, Continuum, NY, 1996).

Columba's entire work is a noble and dignified exposition of themes concerning the creation, the fall, the judgment, and the ultimate destiny of humanity, based on the fundamental views of Columban or Celtic Christianity. The poem was composed in rhyme, probably as an aid to his followers in memorizing the text. In this he was far in advance of his time, for such use of rhyme was new, if not largely unknown in Europe in the sixth century. The structure of the poem is abecedarian in form, consisting of twenty-three verses, each beginning with a letter of the alphabet in order, from A to Z, omitting the letters J, U, and V, as was customary with written texts at that time. This expression of the profound mystery of the Word reflects the Columban Christian's veneration for the alphabet, the Logos, which for them was the epitome of all creative power. Thus the path from Alpha to Zed was a deeply spiritual process, revealed in verbal form by Columba's *Altus Prosator*.

The metric translation that follows was made by Anthony Mitchell and first published in Bishop John Dowden's *The Celtic Church in Scotland* (London, 1894):

Altus Prosator

To The Most High Creator

> Ancient of days, enthroned on high!
> The Father unbegotten He,
> Whom space containeth not, nor time,
> Who was and is and aye shall be:
> And one-born Son, and Holy Ghost,
> Who co-eternal glory share:
> One only God, of persons Three,
> We praise, acknowledge, and declare.

Beings celestial first He made;
Angels and archangels of light,
In Principalities and Thrones,
And mystic rank of Power and Might:
That love and Mystery Divine
Not aimlessly alone might dwell
But vessels have wherein to pour
Full wealth of gifts ineffable.

Cast from the highest heights of heaven,
Far from the angels shining state,
Fadeth from glory Lucifer,
Falling in scorn infatuate.
Angels apostate share his fall,
Steeled with his hate and fired with pride,
Banished from their fellows bright,
Who in the heavenly seats abide.

Direful and foul, the Dragon great,
Whose deadly rage was known of old,
The slippery serpent, wilier
Than living thing that earth doth hold:
From the bright realm of heaven he could,
A third part of the stars entice,
In Hell's abyss to quench their light,
In headlong fall from Paradise.

Earth next and Heaven sea and sky,
Found shape within the Eternal mind,
And stood created. Next appeared
The fruitful herb and trees in kind:
Sun, moon and stars that climb the heavens,
And birds and fishes great and small,
And beasts and herds and living things,
And man to be the king of all.

From every glad Angelic tongue
Soon as the stars sprang into light,
Burst forth the wondering shout that praised
The Heavenly Creation's might.
And, as His handiwork they viewed,
Arose from loving hearts and free
The tribute due of wondrous song,
Swelling in sweetest harmony.

'Gainst Satan's wiles and Hell's assault
Our primal parents could not stand:
And into new abysses fell
The leader and his horrid band:
Fierce forms, with noise of beating wings,
Too dread for sight of mortal eye,
Who, fettered, far from human ken,
Within their prison house do lie.

Him, banished from his first estate,
The lord cast out for evermore:
And now his wild and rebel crew
In upper air together soar.
Invisible lest men should gaze
On wickedness without a name,
And, breaking every barrier down
Defile themselves in open shame.

In the three quarters of the sea
Three mighty fountains hidden lie,
Whence rise through whirling water-spouts
Rich-laden clouds that clothe the sky:
On winds from out his treasure-house
They speed to swell bud, vine and grain,
While the sea-shallows emptied wait
Until the tides return again.

Kings' earthly glory fleeteth fast,
And for a moment is its stay.
God hath all might, and at a nod
The giants fall beneath his sway.
'Neath waters deep with mighty pangs,
In fires and torments dread they rave,
Choked in the whirlpool's angry surge,
Dashed on the rocks by every wave.

Like one that through a sparing sieve
The precious grain doth slowly pour,
God sendeth down upon the earth
The cloud-bound waters evermore:
And from the fruitful breast of heaven,
While changing seasons wax and wane,
The welcome streams that never fail
Pour forth in rich supplies of rain.

Mark how the power of God supreme
Hath hung aloft earth's giant ball,
And fixed the great encircling deep,
His mighty hand supporting all
Upon the pillars which he made,
The solid rocks and cliffs that soar,
And on the sure foundations rest
That stand unmoved for evermore.

None doubteth that within the earth
Glow the devouring flames of hell,
Wherein is prisoned darkest Night
Where noisome beast and serpents dwell,
Gehenna's old and awful moan,
And cries of men in anguish dire,
And falling tears and gnashing teeth,
And thirst, and hunger's burning fire.

Of realms we read beneath the world
Where the departed spirits wait,
Who never cease to bend the knee
To Christ, the only Potentate.
They could not ope the written Book,
Whose seven seals none but He might break,
Fulfilling thus the prophet's word,
That He should come, and victory make.

Paradise and its pleasant glades
From the beginning God did make;
Out of whose fountain-head there flow
Four rivers sweet, earth's thirst to slake;
And midmost stands the tree of life,
With leaves that neither fade nor fall
With healing to the nations fraught,
Whose joys abundant never pall.

Questions the Singer,—"Who hath climbed
Sinai the mountain of the Lord?
The echoing thunders who hath heard,
And ringing trumpet-blast outpoured?
Who saw the lightning's dazzle whirl,
And heaving rocks that crashed and fell,
'Mid meteors glare and darts of flame,
Save Moses, judge of Israel?"

Riseth the dawn:—the day is near.
Day of the Lord, the King of kings;
A day of wrath and vengeance just,
Of darkness, clouds and thunderings;
A day of anguished cries and tears,
When glow of woman's love shall pale;
When man shall cease to strive with man,
And all the world's desire shall fail.

Soon shall all mortals trembling stand
Before the Judge's awful throne,
And rendering the great account,
Shudder each hateful sin to own.
Horror of night! when none can work,
Wailing of men, and flooding tears,
Opening the books by conscience writ,
Riving of hearts with guilty fears.

The trumpet of the archangel first
Shall blare afar its summons dread;
And then shall burst earth's prison bars,
And sepulchres give up their dead.
The ice of death shall melt away,
Whilst dust grows flesh, and bone meets bone,
And every spirit finds again
The frame that was before her own.

Wanders Orion from heaven's height,
To thread his hidden eastern way
—Ere set the gleaming Pleiades—
Through bounds of ocean, day by day;
And Vesper, though his orbit's whirl
Be set twice twelve moons to endure,
One even by ancient paths returns,
—Types both of Him who cometh sure.

Xrist the Most High from heaven descends,
The Cross His sign and banner bright.
The sun in darkness shrouds his face,
The moon no more pours forth her light:
The stars upon the earth shall fall
As figs drop from the parent tree,
When earth's broad space is bathed in fire,
And men to dens and mountains flee.

Yonder in heaven the angel host,
Their ever-ringing anthem raise,
And flash in maze of holy dance,
The Trinity Divine to praise:
The four-and-twenty elders cast
Their crowns before the Lamb on high,
And the four Beasts all full of eyes
Their ceaseless triple praises cry.

Zeal of the Lord, consuming fire,
Shall 'whelm the foes, amazed and dumb
Whose stony hearts will not receive
That Christ hath from the Father come:
But we shall soar our Lord to meet,
And so with Him shall ever be,
To reap the due rewards amidst
The glories of Eternity.

As with St. Benedict, Columba recognized and taught the essential relationship between prayer and daily labor—the religious life and the individual's fulfillment of daily tasks within the community. Thus it is significant that the Columban monks chose the activity of the honey bees and the form of their hives, as the archetypes of their daily life and dwelling places. Columba demonstrated this by precept and personal example, forming the foundation for a truly healthy, balanced life between individual and community. In the religious life this found expression in assembling together for services, daily offices and vigils, in pilgrimages, as well as in prayer, fasting, penance, study, and mediation in their solitary cells.

This active community life of the Columban monks involved among other things, tilling of fields, planting, harvesting, herding, care of the animals, nursing of the elderly and ill, and hospitality to strangers and travelers. This is well expressed in the following lines:

From Erin's shores to Iona's strand,
Columba came to preach and teach and heal,
And found a church which showed the world
How God on earth was real.

In greening grass and reckless wave,
In cloud and ripening corn,
The Celtic Christians traced the course
Of grace through nature borne.

In hosting strangers, healing pain,
In tireless work for peace
They served as servants, Christ their Lord
And found their faith increase.

In simple prayer and alien land
As summoned by the Son,
They celebrated how God's call
Made work and worship one.

God grant that what Columba sowed
Today may harvest yet more seed,
As we engage both flesh and faith
Uniting word and deed.

Thus it becomes clear that Columban Christianity is based upon three fundamentals: learning or knowledge as shown in the human life of thinking; artistic expression stemming from the warmth of heart living in the life of feeling; and the balance of daily prayer and work, manifested in the human being's life of activity. All of this had its development and unfolding on the tiny island of Iona, beginning with the arrival there of Columba and his companions in the year 563.

* * *

One of the Scottish Hebridean islands, Iona is located off the western tip of the Ross of Mull. Peaceful and untroubled it rests, in late afternoon silhouetted by the fading light of the setting sun. Silent it lies, surrounded by the waters of the surging sea, its body of Laurentian granite forming the Atlantic ocean's floor, far beneath the currents of the ever-restless sea, to emerge again into the light of day three thousand miles away in Labrador. This is Iona, home of the resting kings.

As one looks southward from the back of Fingal's Cave on Staffa on a clear day, one's eye can trace the distant outline of Iona, the Isle of Colm-Kill, with its abbey lying below the eastern slopes of Dun-I. A little to the south of the church lies what was described in 1549 by Donald Monro, high dean of the Isles, as "the sepulchre of the best men of all the Isles: the most part of the lords of the isles with their lineage, and of our kings, because it was the most honorable and ancient place that was in Scotland in their days." From the time of Saint Columba this sacred ground has been known as the Reilig Oran, "the burial place of Oran." This entire area with a small chapel nearby (the oldest building extant on Iona), is dedicated to St. Oran, one of Columba's early followers.

Here one can imagine ten or more centuries ago, that at certain times the waters between Mull and Iona were filled with galleys, slowly moving toward the shore, their black sails already partly furled. The sound of voices raised in mourning echoes across the waves, accompanying the transfer of a royal corpse from the ship to the raised ground called Eala, the place of the "song of the dying swan." As was the custom, a solemn gathering of abbot, monks, and vicars came forth to welcome with holy ritual the body of a king of the Isles. Some of these bodies had been brought vast distances over sea and land, coming all the way from the mountains of Norway, from France, others from the gentle green hills of Ireland, as well as from various places in Scotland itself.

What had induced these ships to bear their royal dead to this particular resting place from lands far and near, accompanying the deceased, for whom the following eight days were to be devoted to solemn service and waking? An answer resounds in the words of an ancient Gaelic prophecy:

> Seven years before that last and awful day,
> When time shall be no more,

A watery deluge will o'er sweep
Hibernia's mossy shore.
The green-clad Isla, too, shall sink
While with the great and good,
Columba's happy isle will yet rear
Her hills and towers above the flood.

The days and nights of mourning having been completed, the royal body was reverently, ceremoniously carried along a path across the fields following the "Street of the Dead," leading to the sacred graveyard, the Reilig Oran.

The earliest record of these royal burials begins with an account of the interment of the body of Kenneth MacAlpine, the first king of united Scotland, who reigned in the ninth century. Thenceforward, for the next two hundred years, the ancient chronicles record the burials of the Scottish kings, "the best men of all the Isles," as generally taking place on Iona:

Ruled A.D.

844–860. Kenneth MacAlpine, buried in Iona.

860–863. Donald I, buried in Iona.

863–877. Constantine I, killed in Fife by Norsemen. "They found the king's body," says a later chronicler, Fordun, "and bore it with deep wailing to the island of Iona, where it was enshrined with great honors in his father's bosom."

877–878. Aedh, buried in Iona.

878–889. Girig, buried in Iona at death, after deposition.

899–900. Donald II, killed by Norsemen at Dunottar, buried in Iona.

900–942. (Constantine II, died a Culdee of St. Andrews, and was buried there.)

943–954. Malcolm I, buried in Iona.

954–963. Indulf, buried in Iona, "in the customary tomb of the kings" (Fordun).

963–967. Duff, buried in Iona.

967–971. (Colin, slain by the Britons)

971–995. (Kenneth II, burial unrecorded)

995–997. Constantine III, buried in Iona.

997–1005. (Kenneth III, burial unrecorded).

1005–1034. Malcolm II, buried in Iona.

1034–1040. Duncan, killed by Macbeth, buried in Iona.

1040–1057. Macbeth, buried in Iona.

1057. Lulach the Fatuous, buried in Iona.

1093. Malcolm Canmore (son of Duncan), buried in Iona.

1093–1097. Donald (second son of Duncan), buried in Iona.

Thereafter, Dunfermline followed Iona as the royal burial place of
Scotland.

To Donald Munro, High Dean of the Isles, we owe the following de-
tailed account of his visit to the island of Iona in 1549 (450 years ago):

> Within this isle of Columkill, there is a sanctuary also, or kirkzaird,
> called in Erische, Religoran, quhilk is a very fair Kirkzaird, and
> weill biggit about with staine and lyme: into this sanctuary there is
> 8 tombs of staine, formit like little chapels, with ane braid gray
> marble or quhin staine in the gavil of ilk ane of the tombes. In the
> staine of the ane tombe, there is wretten in latin letters, *Tumulus
> regum Scotie*, that is the tombe or grave of the Scots kinges. Within
> this tombe, according to our Scotts and Erische cronickles, there
> layes forty-eight crowned Scotts kinges, through the quhilk this isle
> has been richlie dotat be the Scotts kinges, as we have saide. The
> tombe on the south syde for said, has this inscription: *Tumulus
> regum Hybernia*, that is the tombe of the Irland Kinges: for, we have
> in our auld Erische cronickles, that there wes 4 Irland kinges eirdit
> in the said tombe. Upon the northe syde of our Scotts tombe, the
> inscriptione beares *Tumulus regum Norwegiae*, that is the tombe of
> the kings of Norroway: in the quhik tombe, as we find in our an-
> cient Erische cronickels, ther layes 8 kinges of Norroway.
>
> Within this sanctuary, also lays the maist part of the Lords of the
> Isles, with their lynage. Twa Clan Lynes, with their lynage, M'Kin-
> non, and M'Guare, with their lynages, with sundrie uthers, inhabi-

tants of the hail isles, because this sanctuary was wont to be the sepulchre of the best men of all the isles, and also of our kinges, as we have said: becaus it was the maist honorable and ancient place that was in Scotland in their days, as we reid.

Thus, according to Munro, within the enclosure of the Reilig Oran lay the remains of forty eight Scottish kings in the middle of the west side, four kings of Ireland at the south, eight Norwegian kings at the north, and one king of France. The fact that historically important individuals from these countries here reveal their origin, bears witness to the widespread activity, faith, and continued effect of Columban Christianity, particularly in the years following the fateful events of the Synod of Whitby in 664, and the subsequent ascendency of Roman Christianity in Britain and Scotland. As one recalls these details of the rich tapestry comprising the history of Iona, the life of St. Columba, the Reilig Oran, burial place of "the best men of all the isles"— "Erin's finest sons" as described by Rudolf Steiner—one can inwardly respond to the words of Fiona Macleod (William Sharp) at the beginning of his essay on Iona:

A few places in the world are to be held holy, because of the *love* which consecrates them, and the *faith* which enshrines them. Their names are themselves talismans of spiritual beauty. Of these is Iona . . . . It is but a small isle, fashioned of a little sand, a few grasses, salt with the spray of an ever-restless wave, a few rocks that wade in heather, and upon whose brows the sea-wind weaves the yellow lichen. But since the remotest days, sacrosanct men have bowed here in worship. In this little island a lamp was lit whose flame lighted pagan Europe, from the Saxon in his fens, to the swarthy folk who came by Greek waters to trade in the Orient. Here Learning and Faith had their tranquil home when the shadow of the sword lay upon all lands from Syracuse, by the Tyrrhene Sea, to the rainy isles of the Orc. From age to age, lowly hearts have never ceased to bring their burthen here. Iona herself has given us for remembrance a fount of youth more wonderful than that which lies under her own boulders of Dun-I. And here *hope* waits. To tell the story of Iona, is to go back to God, and to end in God.

A Concert

Celebrating the 1400th Anniversary
of the Death of St. Columba
in
Dunkeld Cathedral

Saturday 7th June, 1997

52. ABOVE LEFT: Program of concert, showing clachan or monk's ceremonial bell.

53. ABOVE RIGHT: Commemorative stamp for Saint Columba, issued 1997.

54. Seal of the Monastery of Saint Columba.

55. and 56. Saint Martin's Cross, Iona, eighth century: east and west faces.

57. Examples of Celtic manuscript illumination, tenth century.

58. Examples of Celtic manuscript illumination, tenth century.

59. Example of Celtic path of meditation. Manuscript design composed of a single continuous line, illustrating perpetual creation and dissolution of the world. Ireland, seventh century.

60. Saint Oran's Chapel, the Reilig Oran, Iona burial ground.

61. Carved memorial stones, Iona, eighth to tenth century.

Wolffhuegel, pastel blackboard drawing, depicting Christmas event in cave.

William Blake, *Before the Cave of Dante's Inferno*, watercolor, 1827. Copyright Tate Gallery.

Aerial view of the island of Iona.

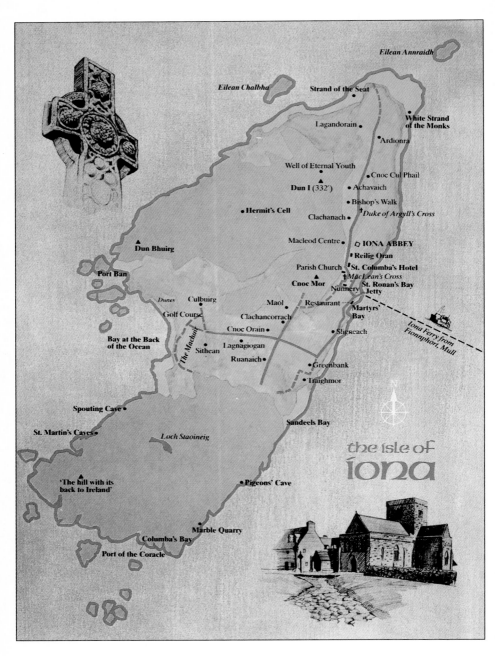

Contemporary map of Iona.

Nicolai Abraham Abildgaard, *The Spirit of Culmin Appears to His Mother*, 1794.

Baron François Gérard (1770-1837), *Ossian, on the Banks of the River Lora, Calls Forth the Spirits of the Heroes of Fingal*, 1801.

Anne-Louis Girodet, *Ossian Receiving the Souls of Napoleon's Generals,*
Malmaison, 1802.

Jean-Auguste Dominique Ingres, *The Dream of Ossian*, watercolor, 1809.

The Poems of Ossian
Enter Today's World

If we look back and see how deeply people were impressed by what they heard about this Fingal's Cave, we shall be able to understand how it was that James Macpherson's revival of these ancient songs in the 18th century made such a mighty impression upon Europe. Nothing can be compared with this impression. Goethe, Herder, Napoleon, harkened to it, and all of them believed they discerned in its rhythms and sounds something of the magic of primeval days. Here we must understand that a spiritual world as it had existed during Fingal's time, arose within their hearts, and they felt themselves drawn to what sounded out of these songs! What was it that thus sounded forth? . . . . Why are the rhythms and sounds of these poems so meaningful, even after being handed down for centuries through tradition alone? They were revived by the Scotsman James Macpherson, so that they can again create for us a consciousness of the connection of the human being with the souls of his ancestors and with the phenomena of Nature

We can understand that this Scotsman experienced in a certain sense a congenial feeling when he described how a line of battle advances, sweeping darkness before it, even as did the spirits who shared in the battle itself. This was in fact something which was able to make a profound impression upon the spiritual-cultural life of Europe. The whole character of the poems, even though presented in a rather free poetical form, awakens in us a feeling for the kind of perception which lived in these ancient peoples. A living knowledge was active in them, a living wisdom concerning the

connection between the spiritual world and the world
of Nature, into which the spiritual world works.
—*Rudolf Steiner, March 3, 1911*

The approaching dawn of the twenty-first century is marked, among
other things, by the renaissance of *The Poems of Ossian*. Following
their first appearance in translation by James Macpherson, London,
1762, they were immediately appreciated and enthusiastically taken
up in a number of countries and fields of art. This enthusiasm continued well into the nineteenth century, culminating in a final echo of response with the publication of the *Centenary Edition of Ossian* in 1896,
edited and introduced by William Sharp (Fiona Macleod), published
by Patrick Geddes and Colleagues, Edinburgh.

Later these Ossianic writings practically disappeared from public attention during almost the entire twentieth century, thus making it especially noteworthy that from 1988 to 1996, three scholarly works
have appeared under the impress of the Edinburgh University Press:

—*The Sublime Savage: A Study of James Macpherson*, by Fiona J
Stafford, 1988.

—*Ossian Revisited*, edited by Howard Gaskill, 1991 (eight essays by
various authors).

—*The Poems of Ossian and Related Works*, edited by Howard Gaskill,
1996 (a definitive edition, including copious reference notes, bibliographical data, indexes, and cross-referencing.)

Meanwhile in 1911, the voice of a single individual was raised in
awareness of the tremendous importance of Ossian as a poet and bard,
of Fingal as an initiate leader, and of the significance of Fingal's Cave
as a place of spiritual enlightenment. This was made manifest in Berlin
on March 3, 1911, when Rudolf Steiner addressed a gathering assembled in the residence of the chief of the general staff Helmuth Von
Moltke, following an orchestral performance of Mendelssohn's Hebridean Overture (Fingal's Cave).

Even more significant than this, in his address Steiner linked the
above three aspects of Ossian, Fingal, and Fingal's Cave with those

whom he called "Erin's finest sons," whose ultimate task would be to bring a knowledge of the Christ impulse to humanity. Thus he was clearly referring to what is known today as Columban or Celtic Christianity. With this unique deed, Steiner created a bridge between *The Poems of Ossian* as they appeared in 1762, and their relevance to our present age and spiritual striving.

James Macpherson, translator of *The Poems of Ossian*, was born in the Highlands of Scotland, near Ruthven, south of Inverness, on October 27, 1736. He studied both at Kings College and Marischal College, Aberdeen, and later at the University of Edinburgh. Upon his return to Ruthven in 1756 he became the local schoolmaster. Soon after this, Macpherson read with interest a letter that appeared in the *Scots Magazine*, together with an English translation of a Gaelic poem. These had been submitted by Jerome Stone, master of the grammar school at Dunkeld, a noted Gaelic student. In reading this, Macpherson's hitherto dormant enthusiasm for Gaelic poetry was awakened and shortly after was intensified when he was introduced to John Home, who encouraged him to translate a number of poems from the Gaelic that had been found in the Highlands. This attracted the attention of Dr. Hugh Blair, minister of the High Church, Edinburgh, and leader of the "Select Circle" of literati, historians, philosophers, and men of letters then active in Edinburgh. Dr. Blair's help and encouragement eventually led to the publication of Macpherson's *Fragments of Ancient Poetry Collected in the Highlands of Scotland*, Edinburgh, 1760.

The success of this book was as instantaneous as it was surprising, and a second edition followed at once. Dr. Blair and his friends then proposed that Macpherson should undertake a journey through the Highlands and Islands of Scotland in order to obtain further material, which they believed had been preserved for centuries by means of oral tradition and retelling. As a result of Dr. Blair's influence and financial support, in December 1761, Macpherson published *Fingal, An Ancient Epic Poem in Six Books, Together with Several Other Poems Composed by Ossian, the Son of Fingal*, translated from the Gaelic language by James Macpherson, London, 1762.

Written in the same musical, measured prose he had used in his earlier volume, it was an immediate success, much greater than Macpherson and his friends could have possibly imagined would be the case.

In fact it speedily became the "book of the moment" in that it triggered off the long overdue Romantic movement throughout the Western world. Clearly, much of Macpherson's material was of his own making, including the fact that at times he confused the stories belonging to the different ancient Iro-Scottish cycles. Nevertheless, the varied sources of his work and any questions as to its authenticity do not alter the fact that he produced a work of literature, which by its deep appreciation of the beauties of nature and the melancholy tenderness of its treatment of the venerable legends, did more than any other single work to bring about the Romantic movement, thus entitling him to be ranked as one of the great writers of Scotland.

Macpherson's later work was divided between political and commercial undertakings. Although he did a considerable amount of further writing, he produced no literary work comparable to *The Poems of Ossian*, written at the age of twenty-five. He ultimately retired to Belleville, his home near Kingussie, where he died on February 17, 1796. His body was later interred with honors in Westminster Abbey, London, not far from Poet's Corner.

To the surprise of everyone, doubtless including Macpherson most of all, the response to the appearance of *Fingal* proved the book to be an international best seller almost overnight, appearing in edition after edition, in country after country, until well into the nineteenth century. While Macpherson's book may have lacked the qualities so dear to the heart of scholars, such as variant readings, variety of mood, copious notes, and the like, he did something else at least equally well worth doing, and he did it superbly. Faithfully and successfully, he presented the qualities of the then little known Ossianic world, bringing it vividly to life in the consciousness of his readers in many countries.

Among a number of British writers who responded with great enthusiasm and were influenced by the appearance of *The Poems of Oss-*

ian were Lord Byron, Samuel Taylor Coleridge, John Keats, William Wordsworth, Percy B. Shelly, Alfred Lord Tennyson, and others. The young Walter Scott, in his own words, "devoured rather than perused" the Ossianic poems and could repeat whole sections of them by heart. The influential English poet and critic William Shenstone (1714–1763) was enthralled by Macpherson's work. Shortly after its publication he suggested that the cause of its popularity was "the public has seen all that art can do, and they want the more striking effects of wild, original, enthusiastic genius. Here is indeed pure original genius, the very quintessence of poetry." Horace Walpole (1717–1797), master of Strawberry Hill, loved *The Poems of Ossian* and praised their imaginative and pictorial nature qualities.

More than one hundred years after the initial publication, Matthew Arnold wrote in *The Study of Celtic Literature*, 1867:

> Make the part of what is forged, modern, tawdry, spurious in the book, as large as you please; strip Scotland, if you like, of every feather of borrowed plumes which, on the strength of Macpherson's *Ossian*, she may have stolen from the true home of Ossianic poetry, Ireland; I make no objection. But there will still be left in the book a residue with the very soul of the Celtic genius in it, and which has the proud distinction of having brought this soul of the Celtic genius into contact with the genius of the nations of modern Europe, and enriched all our poetry by it.

A more mature Sir Walter Scott, while later openly critical of much of Macpherson's work, nonetheless wrote:

> While we are compelled to renounce the pleasing idea that Fingal lived and that Ossian sang, our national vanity may be equally flattered by the fact that a remote and almost barbarous corner of Scotland, produced in the eighteenth century, a bard, capable not only of making an enthusiastic impression on every mind susceptible of poetical beauty, but of giving a new tone to poetry throughout all Europe.

Finally, Bailey Saunders, in his *Life and Letters of James Macpherson*, London, 1895, thus summed up the importance of *The Poems of Ossian*:

> To readers weary of the aridity's of Pope and his school, Macpherson's work presented a striking and impressive picture. This fresh spring of poetic emotion was first opened in English literature in the Ossianic poems; and whatever may be their origin or their history, if they have no other claim to importance, they would deserve it on that ground.

The almost universal commendation following the appearance of *Fingal* (later called *The Poems of Ossian*) was however soon met in certain quarters by a questioning of the authenticity of the sources and authorship of the poems themselves. Thus reactions ranged from total acceptance of the value and genuiness of the work, to outright doubt and rejection of the book as little more that a forgery, the fruit of the poetic efforts and ambition of Macpherson himself. Be that as it may, the effect and widespread influence of *The Poems of Ossian* was immediate and almost breathtaking in its scope and speed, sweeping like a fever through country after country.

One of the evidences of the popularity of *The Poems* is the fact that many people chose for their children names taken from figures appearing in Macpherson's work. One of these was King Bernadotte of Sweden, who out of deference to Napoleon, well-knowing how the emperor treasured the Ossianic poems, named his son Oscar after Ossian's son. Shortly after the birth of her famous son, Lady Jane Wilde, herself a well-known author, wrote to her friends regarding her second son: "he is to be called Oscar Fingal O'Flahertie Wills Wilde. Is that not grand, romantic, misty and Ossianic?"

In addition to the innumerable English editions and translations of *The Poems of Ossian*, which have appeared through the years since 1762, the British Library Catalogue 1991 lists the following foreign language editions:

Italian	1763 to 1826;	8 editions and/or translations
German	1768 to 1940;	15 editions and/or translations
Latin	1769 (specimen translation)	
French	1777 to 1859;	9 editions and/or translations
Russian	1792 and 1928; 2 editions	
Swedish	1794 and 1842; 2 editions	
Spanish	1800 and 1883; 2 editions	
Dutch	1805 to 1845; 3 editions	
Danish	1807 and 1850; 2 editions	
Gaelic	1820	
Bohemian	1827	
Polish	1838	
Greek	1862	
Argentinean	1878	
Hungarian	1833 and 1911; 2 editions	

In Germany, it was above all Johann Wolfgang van Goethe, who, under the influence of his friend, the folklorist Johann Gottfried Herder, was first introduced to Macpherson's work. This interest of Goethe reached its climax in 1773, with his beautiful translation into German of *The Songs of Selma* (these songs later formed the conclusion of the English centenary edition, 1896, edited by William Sharp). The following year, 1774, Goethe included long passages from *The Songs of Selma* in his popular and controversial novel *Die Leiden des Jungen Werthers* [The sorrows of young Werther] published only twelve years after the original appearance of Macpherson's work in English. The following is Goethe's translation of the conclusion of *The Songs of Selma*:

Ich höre den Ruf der Jahre! Sie sagen wie sie vorübergehn, wie? singt Ossian? Bald wird er liegen im engen Haus, kein Barde seinen Ruhm erheben. Rollt hin, ihr dunkelbraunen Jahre, ihr bringt mir keine Freude in eurem Lauf. Eröffnet Ossian sein Grab, denn seine Stärke ist dahin. Die Söhne des Gesangs sind zur Ruhe gegangen, meine Stimme bleibt über wie ein Hauch der fern um den seeumgebene Felsen saust, wenn sich der Sturm gelegt hat. Das finstere Moos rauscht, und aus der Ferne sieht der Schiffer die wallenden Bäume.

Macpherson's English original

I hear the call of years! They say, as they pass along, why does Ossian sing? Soon shall he lie in the narrow house, and no bard shall raise his fame. Roll on, ye dark-brown years, for ye bring no joy on your course. Let the tomb open to Ossian, for his strength has failed. The sons of song are gone to rest: my voice remains like a blast, that roars, lonely, on a sea-surrounded rock, after the winds are laid. The dark moss whistles there, and the distant mariner sees the waving trees.

Friedrich Schiller wrote, à propos of his impression of Ossian, that truer inspiration lay more in the misty mountains and wild cataracts of Scotland than in the fairest of continental meadows and gardens. Johann Gottfried Herder wrote to Goethe, when contemplating a visit to Britain: "How I count on going to the Scots! to Macpherson! where I would fain hear the living songs of a living nation, witness all their influence, see the places that the poems tell of, study in their customs the relics of this ancient world, becoming for a time an ancient Caledonian!" It is reported that Herder even compared Ossian to Moses, and had the *Bible* and *The Poems of Ossian* read to him on his death bed.

As indicated above, the first translation into a foriegn language of *The Poems of Ossian* appeared in 1763 as: *Poesie di Ossian*, antica poeta Celtico, tradotte in prosa Inglese da J. Macpherson, e da quella trasportate in verso Italiano dall' Ab. M. Cesarotti. It was the work of the Abbot Melchior Cesarotti, published in Padova, Italy. It is said that Cesarotti taught himself English in order to translate *The Poems.* He apparently inaugurated a cult of Ossian, and by means of his travels and the excellence of his translation, spread an appreciation of the Ossianic world throughout Italy, to Vienna, and even as far as Warsaw.

It was this translation that was destined to have a profound effect upon Napoleon Bonaparte, who carried its eight volumes with him in his traveling carriage on many of his military campaigns. He later wrote: "*The Poems of Ossian* contain the purest and most animating principles and examples of true honor, courage, and discipline and all the heroic virtues that can possibly exist." In his review of a newly opened exhibition at Fontainebleau, on Bonaparte as a book-lover, Paul Webster in *The Guardian*, London, November 15, 1997, wrote: "the runaway cross-channel favorite (of Bonaparte) was the Italian translation of James Macpherson's eight volumes of *Ossian Highland Legends*." Further, Napoleon founded a Celtic Academy in Paris and commissioned a number of paintings on Ossianic themes by outstanding French artists of the time, for his summer residence at Malmaison.

The Poems of Ossian were also enthusiastically embraced by the French statesman and educator, François René Chateaubriand, in his school. The well-known writer and critic Mme de Staël wrote that: "the word *Romantic* is virtually synonymous with Northern, the poetry of Ossian, as opposed to the Southern, the poetry of Homer."

The fever of enthusiasm for *The Poems of Ossian* quickly spread to the Americas, both south and north, soon after their publication in London, 1762. The first American edition was printed by Thomas Lang in Philadelphia, 1790. Already some years prior to this, Thomas Jefferson (1743–1826), third president of the United States, had imported copies of *The Poems* from booksellers in London, and studied them with great interest, even to the point of learning some Gaelic in order to deepen his understanding of them. It is remarkable that Jefferson, a man so preoccupied with practical details of life and with the natural sciences, should at the same time have been so captivated by this highly imaginative romantic poetry to the point of once unreservedly writing to James Macpherson in 1773: "These pieces have been, and will I think during my life continue to be to me, the source of daily and exalted pleasure. The tender and sublime emotions of the mind were never before so finely wrought up by human hand. I am not ashamed to own that I think this rude bard of the North the greatest poet that has ever existed."

Jefferson's deep regard for the poems clearly came to the fore when he was visited at Monticello in 1782 by the Chevalier de Chastellux, a member of the French Academy and a major general in Rochambeau's army encamped at Williamsburg. In his *Travels in North America in 1780–82*, the Marquis recalls the evening when he and Jefferson shared their mutual interest in Ossian:

> I recollect with pleasure that as we were conversing one evening over a bowl of punch, after Mrs. Jefferson had retired, our conversation turned on the poems of Ossian. It was a spark of electricity which passed rapidly from one to the other; we recollected the passages in those sublime poems which particularly struck us. In our enthusiasm the book was sent for and placed near the bowl, where, by their mutual aid, the night advanced imperceptibly upon us.

According to the researches of Prof. George Friden at the University of Upsala, Sweden, another American who was equally influenced by *The Poems of Ossian* was James Fenimore Cooper (1789–1851). Prof. Friden and his colleagues at Upsala developed the idea that the language of Cooper's Indians was modeled more or less on the style of the Ossianic heroes. This discovery was later described in his essay entitled *James Fenimore Cooper and Ossian*, Upsala, 1949.

Readers of *The Last of the Mohicans* (1826) and other *Leatherstocking Tales* have remarked upon the atmosphere of gloom and melancholy, of "joy in grief," that is present in these novels, an attribute the latter share with Macpherson's Ossian. The destiny of Cooper's Indians is that of the Celtic people in Ossian, where the scattered remnants of a dying world, the glorious past of a people doomed to destruction by an implacable fate, are everywhere present. In Cooper's novels we find the same reflection of past splendor concerning a free, brave, and noble race in times of adversity. The last remaining representatives of the Indians and the Celts submit with melancholy resignation to their inscrutable destiny, to defeats and misfortunes, to the dying out of their people. Hence it can be said that between them, Cooper's Indians and Macpherson's Celts share a common attitude and language: "pure Ossianese."

Cooper's native Americans are idealized in his novels. They are related to Scott's clan chieftains, Byron's pirates, and Ossian's Celtic heroes. All these figures are but phases of the same romantic quality. Cooper saw his Indians in the light of romantic idealism, as the representatives of a dying race, whose days of glory and grandeur are gone forever. He saw them with the same eyes as Macpherson had seen his Celtic heroes in Ossian, as the remnants of a proud people now doomed to destruction by preordained fate, and therefore fitted to take their place in the world of romanticism.

Other American authors influenced by *The Poems of Ossian* include Nathaniel Hawthorne (1804–1864) and Herman Melville (1819–1891), where echoes of heroic themes from the Ossianic poetry are reflected in the titanic scenes in the latter's *Moby-Dick*, 1852. Henry Wadsworth Longfellow (1807–1882) wrote in his journal, 1872: "It came into my head today to read *The Poems of Ossian*, which I have not looked at for a long time—the strange rhapsody, Did not Ossian hear a voice? Or was it the sound of the days that are no more? The Poems are full of the figures of the mist and rain that shroud the northern shores of Scotland."

Yet another American who was intrigued by the poetry of James Macpherson was Walt Whitman (1819–1892) to whom the meeting with *Ossian* was a curious experience. He was particularly intrigued by what he termed Macpherson's prosodic freedom, and even though he half-humoredly referred to him as "a sort of rascal with scamp qualities," nonetheless the influence of his study of *Ossian* demonstratively contributed to the development of his own unique style. This culminated in the publication of *Leaves of Grass* in 1855, which Emerson was to characterize as "the most extraordinary piece of wit and wisdom that America has yet contributed." Whitman felt that he discovered in Macpherson's *Ossian* the same qualities as those he found in the *King James Version of the Bible*, powerfully affected as he was by the latter's different voices, chantings, and rhymical effects.

Ossian and the Fine Arts

⳺ Among the multitude of travelers who have visited Fingal's Cave during the past two centuries, undoubtedly there have been many gifted creative visitors who have drawn inspiration from the architectonic forms of Staffa's caves, as well as from the nature motifs contained in *The Poems of Ossian* themselves.

Appropriately enough, it was in Scotland that Ossianic themes made their first pictorial appearance. Sir James Clerk, third Baronet of

Penicuik near Edinburgh, commissioned the building of a new stately home, including an invitation in 1772 to Alexander Runciman (1736–85) to decorate the ceiling of his great hall with scenes from Ossian. The center of the coved ceiling was occupied by an elliptical compartment showing Ossian singing to Malvina surrounded by a group of listeners, including the spirits of those heroes who had already died. The four corners of the ceiling were devoted to figures allegorically representing the four rivers of Scotland, the Tay, Spey, Clyde, and Tweed, while in the deep cove beneath the ceiling, eleven scenes from the *Poems* themselves were represented. Runciman and his patron saw in these effusions a work of architectural and pictorial art that strove to make the Hall of Ossian a rival to the Sistine Chapel itself! (Unfortunately the hall was destroyed by fire in 1899 and all that remain are some of Runciman's sketches for the themes, now in the National Gallery of Scotland, Edinburgh.)

In Kingussie, not far from Macpherson's birthplace at Ruthven, plans were made in the early nineteenth century to create an "Ossian's Hall." In London, an "Ossian Gallery" was to be erected on an important site, where the great masters of the time were to execute the paintings. Estimates were prepared to promote the scheme and to show how profitable the venture would be. (It is perhaps just as well that neither project was ever realized!)

Meanwhile, on the continent a new style of interior design "à la Ossian" was developed: "gothic windows with ash-gray transparent silk curtains, a hollow oak-like chimney, a desk in the shape of a stone altar, over which would be hung the harp of a bard." Calligraphy and book illustrations were also designed and carried out in what was considered to be an "Ossianic style" by a variety of artists and designers. However it was in the field of painting, more than in any of the other arts, that *The Poems of Ossian* proved to be a prolific source of artistic inspiration. The following are selected examples of paintings based on themes derived from Ossian, and executed in various countries:

1772— Alexander Runciman, *Oscar Singing to Malvina*
1772— Alexander Runciman, *The Death of Oscar*
1772— Alexander Runciman, *Cormac and the Spirit of the Waters*

1773— Angelica Kaufmann, *Trenmor and Inibaca*

1787— Nicolai Abraham Abildgaard, Danish, *Ossian Singing*

1788— Asmus Jacob Carstens, Danish, *Ossian and Alpin's Son*

1792— John Trumbull, American, *Lamderg and Gelchossa*

1796— Asmus Jacob Carstens, *Fingal and the Spirit of Loda*

1797— Josef Anton Koch, Danish, *Fingal and the Spirit of Loda*

1801— François Gérard, French, *Ossian Evoking Ghosts on the Bank of the River Lora*

1802— Anne-Louis Girodet, French, *Ossian Receiving Napoleon's Generals*

1805— Josef Anton Koch, *Death of Ossian*

1805— Philip Otto Runge, German, three character studies of Fingal, Ossian, and Oscar

1805— Philip Otto Runge, eight compositions for the poem *Cathloda*

1813— J. A. D. Ingres, French, *The Dream of Ossian*

1813— J. A. D. Ingres, *Songe d'Ossian*

1830— J. M. W. Turner, sketch, interior of Fingal's Cave

1832— J. M. W. Turner, *Staffa, Fingal's Cave* (oil), exhibited, Royal Academy, London

1912— Victor Vasnetzoff, Russian, *Colma Bewailing the Death of Her Brother and Lover* (apparently this was one of the last paintings to be derived from Ossian)

During the second half of our century two exhibitions of artists' works inspired by Ossian were shown; the first at the Grande Palais in Paris, entitled *Ossian*, Feb.–April 1974, and the second following in the Kunsthalle in Hamburg, May–June in the same year. The latter exhibition was titled *Ossian und die Kunst um 1800*.

The romanticism of *The Poems of Ossian* also left its influence in the world of music, beginning with two operas written in France. The first of these, composed in 1804, was Le Sueur's *Ossian ou Les Bardes*, the second was Méhul's *Uthal*, premiered in 1806, written in the "Ossianic vein." In 1840 the young Danish composer Niels Gade wrote his overture entitled *Echoes of Ossian*, in which he featured the harp as a literal reference to the bard's preferred instrument.

Mendelssohn's Hebridean Overture (*Fingal's Cave*) 1830, has already been discussed above. His second major work on a Scottish theme is his *Scottish Symphony*, 1842, completed two years after the appearance of Gade's overture. It is considered by some musical historians to have been influenced both by Gade's work and by Mendelssohn's visit to Staffa, and to the home of Sir Walter Scott, some eleven years earlier.

Mendelssohn's final encounter with an Ossianic subject was completed in 1846, and premiered in London, March 1847, only a week after Mendelssohn's death. *On Lena's Gloomy Heath* is a setting for bass solo and orchestra, with a text chosen from *Fingal, Book IV*. The sleeping Ossian is awakened by a vision of his deceased wife Everallin, calling upon him to rescue their son, Oscar, who is in mortal danger:

> On Lena's gloomy heath the voice of music died away. The inconstant blast blew hard. The high oak shook its leaves around. Of Everallin were my thoughts, when in all the light of beauty she came; her blue eyes rolling in tears. She stood on a cloud before my sight, and spoke with feeble voice! "Rise Ossian, rise and save my son, save Oscar, prince of men. Near the red oak of Luba's stream he fights with Lochlin's sons."

Two further German composers who occupied themselves with themes from Ossian were Franz Schubert (1797–1828), who in 1815 composed a song cycle based on Harold's and Hummelauer's translation of Macpherson's *Poems*, and Johannes Brahms (1833–1897) whose four songs written in 1860/61, for female voices, Op. 17 are entitled *Songs from Fingal*.

Perhaps no one has more accurately described the continuing effect of James Macpherson's creative work than William Sharp (Fiona MacLeod). He concludes his editor's introduction to the *Centenary Edition of The Poems of Ossian*, 1896, with the following highly perceptive statement: "of this there can be no question: that the ancient poetry, the antique spirit, breathes throughout this eighteenth-century restoration and gives it enduring life, charm, and all the spell of cosmic imagination."

FINGAL,

AN

ANCIENT EPIC POEM,

In SIX BOOKS:

Together with feveral other POEMS, compofed by

OSSIAN the Son of FINGAL.

Tranflated from the GALIC LANGUAGE,

By JAMES MACPHERSON.

Fortia facta patrum.   VIRGIL.

LONDON;

Printed for T. BECKET and P. A. DE HONDT, in the Strand.

MDCCLXII.

62. Title page, first edition, *The Poems of Ossian*, London 1762.

63. From Sir Joshua
Reynolds's oil painting
of James Macpherson,
frontispiece from *The
Poems of Ossian*,
Edinburgh edition, 805.

64. The Reverend
Hugh Blair, Minister
of the High Church,
Edinburgh. Patron
and sponsor of the
literary work of
James Macpherson.

65. George Romney, eminent English painter, portrait of James Macpherson, frontispiece to Bailey Saunders's *Life and Letters of James Macpherson*, London 1895.

66. Johann Wolfgang von Goethe, translator of *The Songs of Selma* into German.

67. Johann Gottfried von Herder, who introduced Goethe to *The Poems of Ossian*.

68. Napoleon Bonaparte, for years an enthusiastic admirer of *The Poems of Ossian*, in the Italian translation by Ab. M. Cesarotti, 1763.

69. Napoleon in his traveling carriage, accompanied by his officers, staff, and his copies of *The Poems of Ossian.*

70. Thomas Jefferson, third president of the United States, a warm admirer of *The Poems of Ossian*. Portrait by Rembrandt Peale.

71. Thomas Jefferson entertaining friends at Monticello, his country estate.

72. James Fenimore Cooper, whose *Leather-stocking Tales* reflect the language of *The Poems of Ossian*.

73. Otsego Hall, home of James Fenimore Cooper, Cooperstown, New York.

74. Walt Whitman, whose fascination with the style of James Macpherson, influenced his *Leaves of Grass*.

75. Alexander Runciman, study for *Ossian Singing to Malvina*, 1772. (By permission of the National Gallery of Scotland)

76. Alexander Runciman, *Death of Oscar, Son of Ossian*. (By permission of the National Gallery of Scotland)

77. Alexander Runciman, *Cormac and the Spirit of the Waters*. (By permission of the National Gallery of Scotland)

78. Alexander Runciman, *God of the River Tweed*. (By permission of the National Gallery of Scotland)

79. Alexander Runciman, *God of the River Spey*. (By permission of the National Gallery of Scotland)

80. The Great Hall of Penicuik House, ceiling paintings by Alexander Runciman, depicting scenes from *The Poems of Ossian*. (By kind permission of Sir John Clerk of Penicuik)

81. Detail of central oval of ceiling in the Great Hall of Penicuik House: *Ossian Singing to Malvina*. (By kind permission of Sir John Clerk of Penicuik)

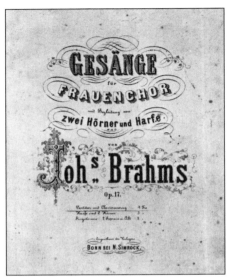

82. Title page of *Four Songs for Women's Choir* by Johannes Brahms, opus 17, 1860.

83. Johannes Brahms's *Song from Fingal*, opus 17, number 4.

84. Niels W. Gade, Danish composer, *Dramatic Poem from Ossian*, ca. 1905.

85. Nicolai Abraham Abildgaard (1743-1809), Danish painter, *Ossian Singing*, 1785.

86. Nicolai Abraham Abildgaard, sketch showing *Fingal and Agandecca*, daughter of the Norwegian leader Starno, 1795.

87. Joseph Anton Koch (1768-1839), Danish painter, *Moon Landscape with Three Ossianic Heroes beside a Fire*, 1800.

88. Joseph Anton Koch, *Cuthullin Leads the Battle*, from *Fingal*, Book I.

89. Joseph Anton Koch, *Darthula's Farewell to Nathos,* from the poem *Darthula,* before 1830.

90. Philipp Otto Runge (1777-1810), self-portrait made for Goethe, Weimar 1806.

91. LOWER LEFT: Philipp Otto Runge, *Sketch of Ossian with His Harp*, 1804/5.

92. LOWER RIGHT: Philipp Otto Runge, *Sketch of Oscar, Son of Ossian*, 1804/5.

93. Philipp Otto Runge, finished pen-and-ink drawing of *Oscar*, 1804/5.

94. Anne-Louis Girodet (1767-1824), *Oscar's Arrival in the Cloud Palace of His Great-Grandfather Trenmor, after the Former's Death* (*Temora, Book II*).

95. Anne-Louis Girodet, *Malvina's Shadow Appears in the Spirit-Hall of Fingal* (Berrathon).

96. Anne-Louis Girodet, *Malvina's Spiritual Being Unites with That of Fingal* (Berrathon).

97. Anne-Louis Girodet, *The Dying Ossian Beholds the Spirit of His Father Fingal* (Berrathon).

98. Etching depicting Ossian with his harp, evoking the spirits of Fingal and his heroes. From the title page of the 1822 edition.

99. Jean-Auguste Dominique Ingres (1780-1867), *The Dream of Ossian*, 1812. "Ossian slumbers while around him the departed heroes descend from the world of the clouds."

Afterword

 In concluding his address given on March 3, 1911, Rudolf Steiner indicated the relationship between human consciousness in Ossian's time and that of today's world, leading into the future:

All this sounded forth out of olden times in the songs about the deeds of the ancient Celts, who fought in mighty battles in order to prepare themselves for further deeds of spiritual life, as we recognize them again today in what the finest sons of the West have achieved. These were the impulses that flowed into the souls of human beings in the eighteenth century, when these ancient songs were revived. It is this which was recalled by those who again saw the wonderful cathedral, built as if by Nature herself, and which led them to say: "Here is a place prepared by destiny, in order that what the bards could sing concerning the deeds of their ancestors, and all that the heroes did to strengthen their forces, could sound back to them as an echo from this temple, which they themselves had no need to build—out of their holy temple, which was built for them by the spirits of Nature and could be a source of inspiration for those who beheld it."

Thus the tones and harmonies of this overture offer an opportunity enabling us to sense, each in our own way, something of the deep mysterious connections which do indeed reign in the history of humankind, of the events which occurred long before our present era on almost the same ground upon which we continue to live today. As it is vital that we deepen ourselves in all that lives within us, and as all that lives within us is but a further resounding of what was present in the past, so this sense for what once existed and today works further in humankind, is of great significance for the spiritual life.

—Rudolf Steiner, March 3, 1911

As one approaches the isle of Staffa and catches a first glimpse of the dark openings of its mysterious great caves, one can begin to experience the result of the creative activity of "that Word," which according to the Gospel of John, has called all things into existence. This perception becomes ever stronger as one observes in closer detail the powerful physical structure of Fingal's Cave itself, through which the subtle working of the Light and Life forces manifest themselves. This is expressed above all in the hexagonal forms of the basaltic columns, bathed as they are in the weaving essence of the Light, and at the same time mirroring the rhythmical rising and falling of the waters of the north Atlantic.

On the other hand, if one attempts to grasp the deeper nature of the working of Life itself, transcending the activity of inorganic forces, one must employ a mode of perception that rises to supersensible insight. A deeper consideration of life as such will make clear that life is doubtless the greatest of all mysteries, for while manifestations of life are everywhere apparent, in reality the very essence of life itself remains hidden from physical perception. In truth, when we penetrate into the realm of life, it is obvious that here we cannot simply continue to use the same methods of understanding that we customarily apply to the inorganic world, but a completely new approach is essential. This approach is set forth in the insights and wisdom given in Anthroposophy, the modern science of spirit, developed in the books and lectures of Rudolf Steiner and related authors.

A deeper understanding of the forces that formed Fingal's Cave, and to which Steiner refers in his address, involves, among other elements, a comprehension of the fourfold nature and working of the etheric formative forces themselves, that is:

- Warmth ether, manifested in the state of creative warmth
- Light ether, manifested in the gaseous state
- Chemical, sound, or number ether, manifested in the fluid state
- Life ether, manifested in the visible elements of the solid state.

An examination of the literature on this subject, some of which is included in the list of books at the end of this book, will readily make clear that the subject of the etheric formative forces involves a profound and far-reaching study, lying beyond the scope of the present work.

In the final sentence of Rudolf Steiner's Address quoted above, he indicates that through gaining an insight into and learning to work creatively with those same forces which enabled Fingal's Cave to come into being, one can today acquire the capacity to recognize something of the potential of these same formative forces. Finally, the possibility exists that these forces will guide human beings naturally and inevitably to meet with courage those exhilarating opportunites and formidable obligations that the future places before us and our world today. Thus the path of evolving human consciousness leads from its earliest manifestation in Communities of the Blood, through those of Head and Heart, to ultimate fulfillment in the Community of all Humanity, a Community in which all humankind may share.

As one leaves Fingal's Cave, following the steep rough-hewn path, one ascends from sea level to a grassy plateau located directly above the cave itself. All around one, the light that shone into the darkness below now bathes the heights of heaven, the sweeping horizon, the very earth itself, in a glory of limitless cosmic effulgence. Here "the Word" which called all things into being, reveals itself in a glorious apotheosis.

The following "Address to the Sun," from Macpherson's rendition of *Carthon*, was Thomas Jefferson's favorite short Ossianic poem. In Jefferson's own words, its nature pictures portray "a warm and moving gospel," exalting human nature, and encouraging us to build a new and idealistic goal for the future of humanity:

Address to the Sun

᭖ O thou that rollest above, round as the shield of my fathers! Whence are thy beams, O Sun! thy everlasting light? Thou comest forth, in thy awful beauty; the stars hide themselves in the sky; the moon, cool and pale, sinks in the western wave. But thou thyself movest alone: who can be a companion of thy course? The oaks of the mountains fall; the mountains themselves decay with years; the ocean shrinks and grows again; the moon herself is lost in heaven; but thou art forever the same; rejoicing in the brightness of thy course. When the world is dark with tempests; when thunder rolls, and lightning flies; thou lookest in thy beauty from the clouds and laughest at the storm. . . .

—from *The Poems of Ossian, Carthon*

Appendix

An Address by Rudolf Steiner

Given in Berlin, following a performance of
Mendelssohn's Hebridean Overture
March 3, 1911

 Through the tones and harmonies of this Hebridean Overture, we have been led in spirit by Felix Mendelssohn to the shores of Scotland, and in our souls, we have thus followed a path, which during the course of human evolution, has been deeply influenced by the secrets of destiny. For from entirely different regions of the Western hemisphere of our earth, as if through a destined current of migration, various peoples were once transplanted into the vicinity of that region, into which this music has now brought us. And by this means, mysterious destinies unfold themselves to us, when we are told, both by what spiritual insight reveals, as well as through outer traces of history, what people experienced in most ancient times in this particular part of the earth.

A memory of the mysterious destinies of those people (inhabitants of the highlands and islands of western Scotland) arose again, as if newly awakened, when in 1772 Fingal's Cave on the island of Staffa belonging to the Hebrides, was visited. Those who beheld it were reminded of mysterious ancient destinies, when they saw how nature itself appeared to have constructed something that may be likened to a wonderful cathedral. It is formed with great regularity, its countless pillars towering aloft, the ceiling arching above constructed of the same stone, while below, the bases of the pillars are washed by the inrushing foaming waves of the sea, which ceaselessly surge and undulate with thunderous music within this mighty temple. Water drips steadily from stone formations above, striking the truncated stumps of the stone below, making melodious magical music. Such phenomena exist there.

Those who upon discovering Fingal's Cave, and who had a feeling for the mysterious things that once took place here, were reminded of that hero, who once upon a time, as one of the most famous individualities of the West, guided destiny here in such a unique manner, and whose fame was sung by Ossian his son, who like Homer, was a blind bard.

If we look back and see how deeply people were impressed by what they heard about this place, we shall be able to understand how it was that James Macpherson's revival of these ancient songs in the eighteenth century made such a mighty impression upon Europe. Nothing can be compared with this impression. Goethe, Herder, Napoleon, harkened to it, and all of them believed they discerned in its rhythms and sounds something of the magic of primeval days. Here we must understand that a spiritual world as it had existed during Fingal's time, arose within their hearts, and they felt themselves drawn to what sounded out of these songs! What was it that thus sounded forth?

To grasp this we must now turn our gaze to those times that coincide with the first impulses of Christianity and the centuries that followed. What happened in the vicinity of the Hebrides, in Ireland and Scotland, in ancient Erin, on the neighboring islands between Ireland and Scotland, as well as in northern Scotland itself? It is there we must seek for the kernel of those peoples of Celtic origin, who had most of all preserved the ancient Atlantean clairvoyance in its fullest purity. The others who had wandered more to the east, having developed further, no longer kept their earlier connection with the ancient gods. In contrast, the Celtic peoples preserved the capacity of experiencing the old clairvoyance, and therefore they were fully immersed in the element of individuality. These people were guided to that particular part of the earth, as if for the accomplishment of a special mission. Here Fingal's Cave, a structure which had been architecturally formed entirely out of the spiritual world itself, stood before them, mirroring their own musical inner depths. We shall imagine these events rightly if we realize that the cave acted as a focus-point, mirroring what lived in the souls of these human beings who, through their destiny, were sent hither as if to a temple built by the spiritual beings themselves. Here those human beings were prepared who later were to receive the Christ Impulse with their full humanity, and were here to undergo something highly unique by way of preparation.

We shall be able to imagine this if we realize that particularly here those ancient folk customs were preserved whereby the tribe was divided into smaller groups based upon family. Those who were related by blood felt themselves closely connected, while all others were looked upon as strangers, were regarded as belonging to another "group-ego." While the migrations from Atlantis toward the east were taking place, those Druid priests who had remained behind in the west, were able to exert a harmonizing influence upon the people living there in small family groups. What they thus gave lived on in the bards who followed them. However, we shall only understand what worked through these bards, when we realize that here the most elementary passions were united with the ancient power of "second sight" into the spiritual world, and that those heroes who at times fought passionately against other clans, perceived impulses coming from the spiritual world that directed them.

Such an active connection between the physical and the soul realms cannot be conceived of today. When a hero raised his sword he believed that a spirit out of the air guided it, and in this spirit he beheld an ancestor who in earlier times had fought upon this same battlefield, and who had gone up yonder in order to help from there. In their ranks both sides felt their ancestors aiding them. However they not only felt them, but also heard them spiritually. It was a wonderful conception that lived in these people: that the heroes had to fight and shed their blood on the battlefield, that after death they ascended into the spiritual world, and that their spirits then vibrated as tone, sounding through the air as spiritual reality.

Those who had proven themselves in battle, but at the same time had trained themselves so that they could listen to what sounded to them out of the spirit as the voice of the past, who were blind to the physical plane, the physical world, no longer able to see the flashing swords, they were nevertheless highly honored. One of these heroes was Ossian. When the warriors wielded their swords, they were aware that their deeds would resound further in the spiritual world, and that bards would later appear who would preserve all this in their songs. This was a living perception to these people.

However, all of this created a quite different conception of humanity than we have today. This earlier conception was based upon the view that the human being was united with spiritual powers sounding forth from the whole world of nature. The human being could not look upon a storm or see a flash of lightning, he could not hear the thunder or the surging of the sea, without sensing that out of all the activities of nature, spirits worked who were connected with the souls of the past, with the souls of his own ancestors. Thus the activity of nature was at that time something altogether different than for us today. Hence the rhythms and sounds of these poems are so meaningful, even after being handed down for centuries through tradition alone. They were revived by the Scotsman James Macpherson, so that they can again create for us a consciousness of the connection of the human being with the souls of his ancestors and with the phenomena of nature.

We can understand that this Scotsman experienced in a certain sense a congenial feeling when he described how a line of battle advances, sweeping darkness before it, even as did the spirits who shared in the battle itself. This was in fact something that was able to make a profound impression upon the spiritual-cultural life of Europe. The whole character of the poems, even though presented in a rather free poetical form, awakens in us a feeling for the kind of perception that lived in these ancient peoples. A living knowledge was active in them, a living wisdom concerning the connection between the spiritual world and the world of nature, into which the spiritual world works.

Out of such wisdom the finest sons from the different clans—that is, those who had the strongest connection with the spirits of the past, who more than others allowed these spirits of the past to live in their deeds—were chosen as a select band. And those who had the strongest clairvoyant forces were placed at its head. This group had to defend the core of the Celtic people against the peoples of the surrounding world. One of these leaders was the clairvoyant hero who has come down to us under the name of Fingal. How Fingal was active in the defense of the ancient spiritual beings against those who wished to endanger them—all of this was handed down in ancient songs, heard out of the spiritual world, the songs of the bard Ossian, Fingal's son, so that it remained alive even into the sixteenth and seventeenth centuries. What Fingal achieved, what his son Ossian heard after Fingal had ascended into the spiritual realms, what their descendants experienced in Ossian's rhythms and sounds, with all this they ever and again ensouled their deeds. This it was that worked on so mightily even into the eighteenth century. And we shall gain a conception of this when we perceive how Ossian lets the voice of his father, Fingal, sound forth in his songs.

In Book IV of *Fingal,* the heroes find themselves in a difficult situation. They are almost overthrown, when new life enters into them (the passages that follow were selected for this Address and were read by Rudolf Steiner from the German translation of *The Poems of Ossian*):

> The King stood by the stone of Lubar. Thrice he reared his terrible voice. The deer started from the fountains of Cromla. The rocks shook on all the hills. Like the noise of a hundred mountain streams, that burst, and roar, and foam! Like the clouds, that gather to a tempest on the blue face of the sky! So met the sons of the desert round the terrible voice of Fingal. Pleasant was the voice of the King of Morven to the warriors of his land. Often had he led them to battle; often returned with the spoils of the foe!
>
> "Come to battle," said the King, "ye children of echoing Selma! Come to the death of thousands. Comhal's son will see the fight. My sword shall wave on the hill, the defense of my people in war. But never may you need it, warriors, while the son of Morni fights, the chief of mighty men! He shall lead my battle, that his fame may rise in song! Oh ye ghost of heroes dead! ye riders of the storm of

Cromla! receive my falling people with joy, and bear them to your hills. And may the blast of Lena carry them over my seas, that they may come to my silent dreams, and delight my soul in rest!". . . .

Now like a dark and stormy cloud edged around with the red lightning of heaven, flying westward from the morning's beam, the King of Selma removed. Terrible is the light of his armor; two spears are in his hand. His gray hair falls on the wind. He often looks back on the war. Three bards attend the son of fame, to bear his words to the chiefs. High on Cromla's side he sat, waving the lightning of his sword, and as he waved we moved. . . .

Fingal at once arose in arms. Thrice he reared his dreadful voice. Cromla answered around. The sons of the desert stood still. They bent their blushing faces to earth, ashamed at the presence of the King. He came like a cloud of rain in the day of the sun, when slow it rolls on the hill, and fields expect the shower. Silence attends its slow progress aloft: but the tempest is soon to arise. Swaran beheld the terrible King of Morven. He stopped in the midst of his course. Dark he leaned on his spear, rolling his red eyes around. Silent and tall Fingal seemed, as an oak on the banks of Lubar, which had its branches blasted of old by the lightning of heaven. It bends over the stream: the gray moss whistles in the wind: so stood the King. Then slowly he retired to the rising heath of Lena. His thousands pour around the hero. Darkness gathers on the hill!

Fingal, like a beam from heaven, shone in the midst of his people. His heroes gather around him. He sends forth the voice of his power. "Raise my standards on high. Spread them on Lena's wind, like the flames of a hundred hills! Let them sound on the winds of Erin, and remind us of the fight. Ye sons of the roaring streams, that pour from a thousand hills, be near the King of Morven! Attend to the words of his power! Gaul, strongest arm of death! O Oscar of the future flights! Connal, son of the blue shields of Sora! Dermid, of the dark brown hair! Ossian, king of many songs, be near your father's arm!" We reared the sunbeam of battle, the standard of the King! Each hero exulted with joy, as, waving, it flew in the wind. It was studded with gold above, as the blue wide shell of the nightly sky. Each hero had his standard too, and each his gloomy men!

Thus Fingal stormed into battle, thus he is described by his son Ossian.

It is therefore no wonder that this life, this consciousness of a connection with the spiritual world, which sank deep into these people, into the souls of the ancient Celts, is the best preparation whereby they were able to spread the personal divine element throughout the west in their own way and from their own soil. For what they had experienced as violent emotions, what they had heard resounding in the melodies of the spiritual world, prepared them for a later time when they were to bring into the world sons who revealed these emotions in their souls in a purified and milder form. Thus we may say—it appears as if at that later time Erin's finest sons again heard the voices of their ancient bards singing of what they once had heard out of the spiritual world as the deeds of their forefathers, but it was as if in Erin's finest sons the ancient battle cries had now been reshaped and clarified, and had become words that could express the greatest Impulse of humankind.

All this sounded forth out of olden times in the songs about the deeds of the ancient Celts, who fought in mighty battles in order to prepare themselves for further deeds of spiritual life, as we recognize them again today in what the finest sons of the West have achieved. These were the impulses that flowed into the souls of human beings in the eighteenth century, when these ancient songs were revived. It is this that was recalled by those who again saw the wonderful cathedral, built as if by nature herself, and which led them to say: "Here is a place prepared by destiny, in order that what the bards could sing concerning the deeds of their ancestors, and all that the heroes did to strengthen their forces, could sound back to them as an echo from this temple, which they themselves had no need to build—out of their holy temple, which was built for them by the spirits of nature and which could be a source of inspiration for those who beheld it."

Thus the tones and harmonies of this overture offer an opportunity enabling us to sense, each in our own way, something of the deep mysterious connections that do indeed reign in the history of humankind, of the events that occurred long before our present era on almost the same ground upon which we continue to live today. As it is vital that we deepen ourselves in all that lives within us, and as all that lives within us is but a further resounding of what was present in the past, so this sense for what once existed and today works further in humankind, is of great significance for the spiritual life.

Acknowledgments

In preparing this book, the authors wish to express their deep appreciation to the late Marion Cathcart Millet of Edinburgh, who over many years awakened in them an awareness, love, and enthusiasm for Scotland, its folkore, history, and natural beauty.

The authors also wish to express their thanks and appreciation to the following individuals, whose immediate readiness in responding to their needs has been of great assistance in assembling and authenticating much of the material included in this book: first of all, to James Pratt, information services, and to Alison Rosie, assistant librarian, both of Aberdeen Central Library; to Erdmute Lloyd, librarian, Goethe Institute, London; to Angela Craig-Fournes of Berlin; and to Alastair de Watteville, former owner of Staffa and author of *The Island of Staffa* (1993).

Above all, however, the authors are particularly grateful for the constant personal encouragement, and interest in the material included in this book, shown by Gene Gollogly of The Continuum Publishing Company.

Select Bibliography

Allen, Paul M., & Joan de Ris Allen. *The Time Is at Hand*. Anthroposophic Press, N.Y. 1995.

Allen, Paul M. *A Christian Rosenkreutz Anthology*. Rudolf Steiner Publications, N.Y. 1968.

Beckh, Hermann. *Ätherische Bildekräfte und Hieroglyphen*. Gäa-Sophia, Dornach. 1926.

Bradley, Ian. *Columba, Pilgrim and Penitent*. Wild Goose Publications, Glasgow. 1996.

Curtin, Jeremiah. *Myths and Folk Tales of Ireland*. Dover Publications, N.Y. 1975.

Gaskill, Howard, ed. *Ossian Revisited*. Edinburgh University Press. 1991.

——, ed., *The Poems of Ossian*. Edinburgh University Press. 1996.

Gregory, Lady Augusta. *Gods and Fighting Men*. Colin Smythe Ltd., Gerrards Cross. 1970.

Hagemann, Ernst. *Weltenäther-Elementarwesen-Naturreiche*. Novalis Verlag, Schaffhausen. 1987.

Lehrs, Ernst. *Man or Matter*, Rudolf Steiner Press, London. 1993.

MacCulloch. Donald. *The Wondrous Isle of Staffa*, 4th Edition. 1975.

MacKenzie. Henry, Chairman. *Report of Highland Society*. Edinburgh. 1805.

Menzies, Lucy. *St. Columba of Iona*. 1920, JMF Books, facsimile edition reprint. 1992.

Merry, Eleanor. *The Flaming Door*. New Knowledge Books, London. 1962.

O'Brien, Henry. *Atlantis in Ireland*. London. 1834. Steinerbooks, N.Y. 1992.

Okun, Henry. "Ossian in Painting," *Journal of the Warburg and Courthauld Institute*. London. 1967. (pp. 327–356).

Saunders, Bailey, *Life and Letters of James Macpherson*, London. 1894.

Schure, Edouard. *From Sphinx to Christ, An Occult History*. Rudolf Steiner Publications. 1970.

————. *The Great Initiates*. Rudolf Steiner Publications, N.Y. 1961.

Sharp, William (Fiona Macleod), ed., *The Poems of Ossian, Centenary Ed.*, Patrick Geddes, Edinburgh. 1896.

Stafford, Fiona. *The Sublime Savage*. Edinburgh University Press. 1988.

Steiner, Rudolf. *Evolution of Consciousness*. Rudolf Steiner Publications, London. 1966.

————. *Mystery Centers*. Spiritual Research Editions, Blauvelt, N.Y. 1989.

————. *Mysticism at the Dawn of the Modern Age*. Rudolf Steiner Publications. 1960.

Streit, Jakob. *Sun and Cross*. Floris Books, Edinburgh. 1984.

Trenholme, Rev. E. C. *The Story of Iona*. Douglas, Edinburgh. 1909.

Wachsmuth, Guenther. *Etheric Formative Forces in Cosmos, Earth and Man*. Anthroposophic Press. London and New York. 1932.

————. *Evolution of Mankind*. Philosophic-Anthroposophic Press. Dornoch. 1961.

Watteville, Alastair de. *The Island of Staffa*. Romsey Fine Art. 1993.